I0696960

HOW TO BE A GOOD CONVERSATIONALIST

DAVID SANDUA

"The greatest skill of a good conversationalist is active listening. Knowing how to listen is an art that transforms relationships".

Martin Luther King Jr.

INDEX

I. INTRODUCTION

A good conversationalist is someone who possesses the ability to engage in meaningful and engaging discussions with others. Being able to hold a conversation is a valuable skill that can contribute to personal growth, professional success, and the development of meaningful connections and relationships. In our increasingly connected and fast-paced world, the art of conversation is often neglected, as people turn to digital communication and social media platforms to interact with others. These forms of communication lack the depth and nuance of a face-to-face conversation. Thus, it becomes imperative for individuals to develop the skills necessary to become good conversationalists. The purpose of this essay is to explore the nuances of being a good conversationalist and provide tips and strategies for improving conversational skills. Conversations not only serve as an avenue for information exchange but also provide an opportunity for individuals to learn from others' perspectives, challenge their own beliefs, and develop critical thinking skills. Being able to engage in meaningful conversations also helps individuals to navigate conflicts and disagreements in a respectful and productive manner. Being a good conversationalist goes beyond the ability to talk eloquently; it involves active listening and genuine interest in what others have to say. Active listening entails giving one's full attention to the speaker and making a conscious effort to comprehend and engage with their words. This includes maintaining eye contact, nodding or providing verbal cues to show understanding, and avoiding distractions such as checking one's phone or thinking about one's response instead of actively listening. Genuine interest, on the other hand, involves valuing the thoughts and opinions of others and being open to learning from them, regardless of whether one agrees with them or not. It requires setting aside personal biases and judgments and approaching conversations with an open mind. Good conversationalists are mindful of their body language and verbal cues. Body language, including facial expressions, gestures, and posture, can convey a person's level of interest, engagement, and understanding. Verbal cues such as asking questions, summarizing the speaker's points, and providing thoughtful responses also demonstrate active engagement in the conversation. Good conversationalists are aware of the appropriate timing and turn-taking during conversations. They recognize when it is appropriate to speak and when it is necessary to allow others to express themselves. Interrupting or monopolizing a conversation can be viewed as rude and disrespectful, hindering the development of meaningful exchanges. Developing good conversational skills is a continuous and iterative process that requires practice, self-reflection, and an openness to feedback. By making a conscious effort to be present, actively listen, and engage in conversations with genuine interest, individuals can enhance their ability to connect with others on a deeper level. Being a good conversationalist is an essential skill in today's society. It involves active listening, genuine interest, mindful body language and verbal cues, and being aware of appropriate timing and turn-taking. By nurturing these qualities, individuals can improve their conversational skills, fostering the development of meaningful connections, and enriching their personal and professional lives.

DEFINITION OF A GOOD CONVERSATIONALIST

A good conversationalist can be defined as an individual who possesses a set of skills and qualities that enable them to engage in meaningful and effective conversations. Firstly, a good conversationalist is someone who actively listens to others. They pay attention to the speaker's words, body language, and emotions, demonstrating genuine interest in what the other person has to say. Active listening involves providing verbal and non-verbal cues, such as nodding, maintaining eye contact, and offering encouraging remarks, which not only show respect but also make the speaker feel valued. Secondly, a good conversationalist is highly empathetic. They have the ability to understand and share the feelings of others, which allows them to connect on a deeper level. By showing empathy, they create a safe and comfortable environment that encourages open and honest conversations. A good conversationalist possesses excellent communication skills. They are articulate and express their ideas and thoughts clearly, making it easy for others to understand and engage in the conversation. Good conversationalists are skilled at asking thoughtful and open-ended questions that prompt meaningful discussions. These questions not only encourage the speaker to expand on their ideas but also demonstrate a genuine curiosity and desire to learn more. A good conversationalist knows and understands the importance of non-verbal communication. They are aware of their own body language and use it effectively to express interest, attentiveness, and enthusiasm. They are also skilled at reading the non-verbal cues of others, allowing them to adjust their approach and adapt to the speaker's mood or preferences. Another defining trait of a good conversationalist is their ability to respect and value differing opinions. They understand that not everyone will share the same views or perspectives and embrace these differences as an opportunity for enriching discussions. They listen attentively to opposing viewpoints, without judgment or prejudice, and engage in constructive debates, fostering a culture of mutual understanding and intellectual growth. A good conversationalist knows and respects the importance of timing and balance. They are aware of when to speak and when to listen. They give others equal opportunities to participate in the conversation and avoid dominating the discussion or interrupting others. They maintain a balanced exchange of ideas, ensuring that all participants feel heard and valued. A good conversationalist possesses a combination of active listening skills, empathy, effective communication, the ability to ask thoughtful questions, non-verbal communication awareness, respect for differing opinions, and a sense of timing and balance. By honing these skills and qualities, one can become a good conversationalist, fostering meaningful and engaging conversations that leave a lasting positive impression on all participants.

IMPORTANCE OF BEING A GOOD CONVERSATIONALIST

One of the key reasons why being a good conversationalist is important is because it enhances our personal and professional relationships. In our personal lives, being able to engage in meaningful conversations allows us to connect with others on a deeper level. It helps us build rapport, establish trust, and foster stronger bonds with friends, family, and romantic partners. When engaging in discussions, whether it be about our interests, experiences, or opinions, being a good conversationalist allows us to authentically express ourselves, while also respecting and valuing the perspectives of others. By actively listening and engaging in reciprocal dialogue, we demonstrate a genuine interest in the people we interact with, making them feel heard and understood. Being a good conversationalist is not only crucial in personal relationships but also in our professional lives. The ability to effectively communicate and engage in conversations is highly valued in the workplace, as it fosters collaboration, understanding, and productivity among colleagues. In team settings, being able to articulate ideas clearly, actively listen to others' viewpoints, and contribute to discussions thoughtfully is essential for effective problem-solving and decision-making. Good conversational skills are crucial in networking and building professional relationships. By being able to engage in meaningful and insightful conversations with colleagues, mentors, or potential employers, we can make a lasting impression and open doors to new opportunities. Being a good conversationalist also helps us navigate and thrive in diverse contexts, whether it be in social gatherings, community events, or even when traveling. Conversations are a fundamental aspect of human interaction, and being able to communicate effectively with individuals from different backgrounds, cultures, and perspectives is essential for fostering mutual understanding and bridging cultural gaps. Good conversational skills enable us to learn from others, expand our horizons, appreciate different viewpoints, and develop empathy. In today's fast-paced world, where technology and social media increasingly dominate our interactions, the importance of being a good conversationalist becomes even more crucial. Genuine and meaningful conversations foster human connection, which is vital for our overall well-being. While social media platforms offer us the opportunity to stay connected with others, they often lack the depth and authenticity that comes with face-to-face conversations. By being a good conversationalist, we can break through the barriers of virtual communication and truly connect with others on a more profound level.

Being a good conversationalist is of significant importance in various aspects of our lives, including personal relationships, professional success, and cultural understanding. It allows us to build stronger connections with others, collaborate effectively in the workplace, navigate diverse contexts, and foster mutual understanding. By actively listening, engaging in reciprocal dialogue, and expressing ourselves thoughtfully, we can enhance the quality of our interactions, thereby enriching our lives and the lives of those around us.

OVERVIEW OF THE ESSAY

In this essay, we have explored some essential aspects of becoming a good conversationalist. We began by acknowledging the significance of effective communication skills and the ability to engage in meaningful conversations. Building upon this foundation, we then delved into the importance of listening actively and attentively. We understood that listening goes beyond just hearing; it involves making a conscious effort to understand and empathize with the speaker. We discussed the significance of maintaining eye contact and maintaining an open-body posture to show interest and respect for the speaker. We examined the role of nonverbal cues, such as facial expressions and gestures, in enhancing the effectiveness of our conversations. By being aware of and utilizing these nonverbal cues appropriately, we create a comfortable and inviting environment for others to express their thoughts and feelings freely. We have emphasized the need for developing empathy and emotional intelligence, as these qualities play an integral role in establishing meaningful connections with others. We have explored the power of validating others' emotions, demonstrating understanding, and offering support when engaging in conversations. Through empathy, we not only strengthen our relationships but also foster an inclusive and supportive environment. We have acknowledged the importance of managing our own emotions during conversations, as unchecked emotions can hinder our ability to communicate effectively. By practicing self-awareness and emotional self-regulation, we avoid conflicts and promote healthy dialogue. We have discussed the value of being authentic and genuine in our interactions. By being true to ourselves, we show others that we are trustworthy and reliable conversational partners. This authenticity fosters a sense of connection and fosters the development of long-lasting relationships. This essay has provided a comprehensive overview of the fundamental principles of becoming a skilled conversationalist. From active listening to nonverbal cues, empathy to emotional management, and authenticity to genuine expression, these aspects collectively contribute to engaging in meaningful and impactful conversations. It is crucial to recognize that becoming a good conversationalist requires constant practice, patience, and a willingness to continually learn and improve. By embracing these principles and integrating them into our daily interactions, we can enhance not only our personal relationships but also our professional endeavors. Conversations are the building blocks of society, and by becoming better conversationalists, we contribute to a more positive and connected world. A good conversationalist understands the importance of active listening and responding with empathy. Engaging in conversation requires more than just speaking; it entails truly listening to the other person's words and feelings. By actively listening, one acknowledges the speaker's perspective and validates their experience. This involves maintaining eye contact, nodding in agreement, and asking clarifying questions when needed. Active listening allows one to better understand the speaker's point of view and build deeper connections. Responding with empathy is crucial for effective communication. Good conversationalists recognize that emotions play a significant role in human interaction and are attentive to the speaker's emotions. They practice empathy by putting them-selves in the other person's shoes, understanding their feelings, and responding compassionately. This fosters trust, openness, and understanding, creating an environment where both parties feel heard and valued. In addition to active listening and empa-thy, a good conversationalist possesses the ability to ask thoughtful and meaningful questions. Thoughtful questions en-courage further discussion, delve into the depths of a topic, and demonstrate genuine interest. Open-ended questions are partic-ularly effective for this purpose as they encourage the speaker to elaborate, share their thoughts, and develop their ideas. These questions invite the speaker to contribute more to the conversation, thereby enriching it. By asking thoughtful ques-tions, a good conversationalist not only shows their engagement but also encourages the other person to open up and actively participate. Being a good conversationalist necessitates being mindful of one's own body language and non-verbal cues. Com-munication is not limited to words alone; it also encompasses gestures, facial expressions, and body language. A good con-versationalist ensures that their non-verbal cues align with their spoken words, signaling openness, attentiveness, and respect. They maintain a relaxed and open posture, leaning in slightly to show interest and engagement. They use appropriate facial ex-pressions to convey understanding and empathy, such as a nod, a smile, or a concerned look. Being aware of one's non-verbal cues is essential, as they can either enhance or detract from the overall message being conveyed. A good conversationalist un-derstands the importance of balancing speaking and listening. While actively listening is crucial, it is equally important to con-tribute to the conversation. Engaging in a dialogue requires sharing experiences, thoughts, and opinions. A good conversationalist does not dominate the conversation; they strike a balance between speaking and listening, ensuring that both parties have an equal opportunity to express themselves. This allows for a dynamic and interactive conversation, fostering a sense of mutual respect and understanding between the participants.

Being a good conversationalist involves actively listening, responding with empathy, asking thoughtful questions, being mindful of body language, and balancing speaking and listening. By mastering these skills, individuals can become effective communicators, fostering meaningful connections and building stronger relationships. Conversations are the building blocks of human interaction, and a good conversationalist holds the key to unlocking the potential of these interactions.

II. ACTIVE LISTENING SKILLS

Active listening skills are crucial for being a good conversationalist. Active listening involves fully engaging in the conversation, not just hearing the words being said but also understanding and empathizing with the speaker's thoughts and feelings. To practice active listening, one must ensure that their focus is solely on the speaker and what they are saying, rather than being distracted by their own thoughts or external factors. Active listening entails providing verbal and nonverbal cues to show that one is paying attention and genuinely interested in what the speaker has to say. One important aspect of active listening is maintaining eye contact. Looking directly at the speaker demonstrates that one is fully present in the conversation and ready to listen. It also allows one to observe the speaker's nonverbal cues, such as facial expressions and body language, which can provide valuable additional information about the speaker's thoughts and emotions. For example, if the speaker appears excited or passionate about a particular topic, maintaining eye contact and nodding in agreement can encourage them to continue sharing their thoughts.

Active listening involves practicing empathy and understanding. This means putting oneself in the speaker's shoes and trying to comprehend their perspective, even if one might not agree with it. By actively listening and empathizing, one can validate the speaker's feelings and experiences, which can foster a more open and genuine conversation. Responding with statements such as, "I understand how you feel" or "That must have been difficult for you" can show that one truly cares about what the speaker is sharing. Seeking clarification is another crucial active listening skill. It is important to ask questions or seek further information when one is unsure about something the speaker has said, ensuring that both parties are on the same page. This not only shows that one is engaged in the conversation but also helps to prevent misunderstandings and allows for a deeper, more meaningful exchange. In addition to nonverbal cues, active listening involves providing verbal feedback, such as nodding, summarizing what the speaker has said, or acknowledging their thoughts and ideas. This active participation conveys that one is actively processing the information being shared and that their input is valued. Summarizing the speaker's main points can help to ensure that one has understood the conversation correctly and can lead to further discussion or exploration of the topic. Active listening skills are essential for building rapport and establishing meaningful connections with others. By fully engaging in conversations and actively listening to the thoughts and feelings expressed by others, one can foster more fulfilling and rewarding interactions. Active listening can lead to increased understanding, empathy, and the exchange of diverse perspectives, contributing to personal growth and the development of well-rounded conversational skills. By honing active listening skills, one can become a more effective and empathetic communicator, strengthening both personal and professional relationships.

PAYING ATTENTION TO THE SPEAKER

Paying attention to the speaker is a crucial aspect of being a good conversationalist. In today's fast-paced and distraction-filled world, it is common for individuals to lose focus easily during conversations. Actively listening and being fully present in the conversation is vital for effective communication. One way to pay attention to the speaker is by maintaining eye contact. By looking directly at the person who is speaking, it signals to them that they have your undivided attention and that you are genuinely interested in what they have to say. Maintaining eye contact demonstrates respect and helps to establish a deeper connection with the speaker. Another important aspect of paying attention to the speaker is by being mindful of non-verbal cues. These cues include nuances in facial expressions, gestures, and body language, which can often convey emotions and thoughts more profoundly than words alone. By paying attention to these cues, a good conversationalist can pick up on underlying messages or feelings that the speaker may not explicitly express. Actively listening and responding to the speaker's words is an essential part of paying attention. It involves being fully present in the conversation, focusing on what is being said, and asking relevant questions or providing thoughtful responses. This not only demonstrates that you are engaged in the conversation but also encourages the speaker to continue sharing their thoughts and ideas. Paraphrasing and summarizing what the speaker has said can show that you are actively listening and attempting to understand their perspective. This can further foster an open and respectful dialogue. Limiting distractions is crucial when paying attention to the speaker. In today's digital age, it is easy to be distracted by notifications, incoming messages, or the urge to check one's phone. Being fully present in the conversation requires setting aside distractions and giving one's undivided attention to the speaker. This may involve finding a quiet and secluded space to converse or turning off electronic devices to minimize disruptions. By eliminating distractions, a good conversationalist can demonstrate respect for the speaker and create an environment that encourages open and meaningful dialogue. Paying attention to the speaker is essential for effective communication and being a good conversationalist. It involves maintaining eye contact, being mindful of non-verbal cues, actively listening and responding to the speaker's words, paraphrasing and summarizing their thoughts, and limiting distractions. By incorporating these practices, individuals can enhance their communication skills and foster deeper connections with others. Paying attention to the speaker allows for a more open and respectful dialogue, where ideas can be shared, and understanding can be cultivated.

MAINTAINING EYE CONTACT

Maintaining eye contact is a crucial aspect of being a good conversationalist. It signifies attentiveness and interest in the speaker, conveying respect and establishing a connection. When engaged in a conversation, the ability to hold eye contact demonstrates that one is actively listening and focused on the speaker's words. In Western cultures, maintaining eye contact is generally considered a sign of trustworthiness, sincerity, and confidence. By looking directly into someone's eyes, we are able to gauge their emotions, intentions, and sincerity, allowing us to respond more effectively and authentically. Eye contact also plays a significant role in nonverbal communication, complementing the verbal message and enhancing the overall understanding of the conversation. Maintaining eye contact can be challenging for some individuals due to various reasons such as cultural differences, shyness, anxiety, or lack of confidence. In some cultures, avoiding eye contact is a sign of respect or modesty, and prolonged eye contact may be considered inappropriate or confrontational. Thus, it is essential to consider cultural norms and adapt one's behavior accordingly to ensure effective communication. Shyness or anxiety can make it difficult to maintain eye contact, causing one to divert their gaze or look away frequently. Overcoming these barriers requires conscious effort and practice, as it can greatly enhance one's ability to engage in meaningful conversations. Eye contact is a powerful tool for establishing rapport and developing connections with others. By maintaining eye contact, we create a sense of intimacy and trust, fostering a deeper level of engagement in the conversation. When both individuals are engaged in maintaining eye contact, it signals mutual respect and interest, leading to a more fulfilling and productive dialogue. The act of looking someone in the eye can also be empowering and empowering oneself, instilling confidence and exhibiting assertiveness. This is especially important in professional settings, as strong eye contact can help one make a lasting impression and be perceived as competent and trustworthy. It is worth noting that maintaining eye contact shouldn't be mistaken for staring or prolonged gazing, as this can make the other person uncomfortable or intimidated. The goal is to strike a balance between maintaining eye contact without causing discomfort or distraction. It is recommended to periodically break eye contact, allowing natural moments for the eyes to rest or shift focus briefly. This helps create a relaxed and natural flow to the conversation, preventing any undue tension or unease. Maintaining eye contact is a fundamental aspect of being a good conversationalist. It demonstrates active listening, respect, and interest in the speaker. It aids in nonverbal communication, enhances understanding, and fosters connections with others. While cultural differences, shyness, or anxiety can present challenges to maintaining eye contact, overcoming these barriers can greatly improve communication skills and overall conversational abilities. By practicing the art of maintaining eye contact, individuals can develop stronger connections, establish trust, and become more effective communicators.

AVOIDING DISTRACTIONS

In addition to actively listening and showing interest in the conversation, another important aspect of being a good conversationalist is the ability to avoid distractions. In today's hyperconnected world, distractions are everywhere, ranging from smartphones and social media notifications to background noise and wandering thoughts. To truly engage in a meaningful conversation, it is essential to minimize these distractions and give our undivided attention to the person we are conversing with.

One common distraction that plagues our conversations is the excessive use of smartphones. We have all experienced moments when we are engrossed in a stimulating discussion only to be interrupted by the irresistible temptation of checking our phones. Whether it is to respond to messages or simply mindlessly scrolling through social media feeds, this behavior sends a clear message to the other person: our conversation is not as important as what is happening on our screens. To avoid this distraction, it is crucial to silence or put away our phones when engaging in a conversation. By doing so, we demonstrate our respect and commitment to the interaction, which creates a more conducive environment for a fruitful dialogue.

External noises and interruptions can also hinder our ability to be fully present in a conversation. Background noises in a coffee shop, for instance, can often make it difficult to focus on the person's words, leading to misunderstandings or the need for constant repetition. To combat this distraction, finding a quieter environment or using noise-canceling headphones can significantly enhance the quality of the conversation. Minimizing other potential disruptions such as turning off the television or music can further eliminate unnecessary distractions, allowing both parties to fully immerse themselves in the exchange of ideas.

Our own wandering thoughts and preoccupations can also pose challenges to maintaining focus during a conversation. It is not uncommon for our minds to drift away, especially when the topic at hand does not immediately capture our interest or relates to our personal concerns. Allowing our thoughts to wander not only impedes the conversation but also shows a lack of genuine engagement and respect for the other person. Rather than succumbing to these distractions, we must consciously redirect our attention to the conversation at hand. This can be achieved by actively reminding ourselves to listen attentively, asking clarifying questions, and showing empathy, regardless of our personal interests or concerns. Avoiding distractions is a vital skill that every good conversationalist should develop. By minimizing the use of smartphones, finding suitable environments, and controlling our wandering thoughts, we can foster an atmosphere of undivided attention and genuine engagement in our conversations. This not only enhances the quality of our interactions but also demonstrates our respect and commitment to the person we are conversing with. In a world filled with endless distractions, being able to give our full focus to another individual is a valuable and increasingly rare ability. By honing this skill, we can truly become exceptional conversationalists and create deeper connections with those around us.

DEMONSTRATING GENUINE INTEREST

In addition to being a good listener and asking thoughtful questions, demonstrating genuine interest in the conversation is another key aspect of being a good conversationalist. When engaging in a conversation, it is essential to show the other person that you are not just passively listening, but actively participating and interested in what they have to say. One way to do this is through non-verbal cues, such as maintaining eye contact, nodding your head, and displaying open body language. These gestures signal to the speaker that you are fully present in the conversation and genuinely interested in what they are saying.

Verbal cues can also be used to convey genuine interest in a conversation. This can be done by providing appropriate feedback and responses, such as expressing empathy or excitement when appropriate. By doing so, you demonstrate that you are actively engaged and emotionally invested in the conversation. For instance, if someone is sharing a personal success or accomplishment, responding with genuine enthusiasm and congratulations can make the speaker feel valued and appreciated.

Another important aspect of demonstrating genuine interest is avoiding distractions. In today's digital age, it is easy to get distracted by notifications and messages on our phones, but this can significantly hinder the flow and quality of a conversation. To truly show genuine interest, it is crucial to put away distractions and give one's undivided attention to the speaker. This not only shows respect for the conversation but also allows for a deeper and more meaningful exchange of ideas.

Demonstrating genuine interest also involves active engagement with the topic at hand. This means taking a genuine interest in the subject being discussed, asking follow-up questions when appropriate, and sharing relevant personal experiences or insights. By demonstrating an active engagement with the topic, you show that you are intellectually invested and genuinely interested in learning more. This can help foster a deeper connection between the speaker and the listener, creating a more meaningful and enjoyable conversation for both parties.

Demonstrating genuine interest also means being willing to explore different perspectives and ideas. It is natural for conversations to involve differing opinions and viewpoints, but a good conversationalist approaches these moments with an open mind and a genuine curiosity to understand the other person's viewpoint. This can be done by actively listening to their arguments, asking thoughtful questions, and acknowledging the validity of their perspective. By doing so, you demonstrate respect for the other person's thoughts and create an environment where meaningful dialogue can take place.

Demonstrating genuine interest is an essential aspect of being a good conversationalist. By showing non-verbal cues, providing appropriate feedback and responses, avoiding distractions, actively engaging with the topic, and being open to different perspectives, one can create an atmosphere of genuine interest and respect. Genuine interest fosters deeper connections, promotes meaningful dialogue, and enhances the overall quality of conversations. It is worth cultivating this skill to become a better conversationalist.

NODDING AND RESPONDING APPROPRIATELY

Nodding and responding appropriately is crucial for being a good conversationalist. It shows the speaker that you are engaged and actively listening to what they are saying. Nodding can indicate agreement or understanding, which can encourage the speaker to continue and feel validated in their thoughts and ideas. On the other hand, failing to nod or respond appropriately can give the impression of disinterest or boredom, which can have a detrimental effect on the conversation. Responding appropriately involves providing relevant and thoughtful feedback to the speaker. This can come in the form of asking clarifying questions, offering insights or alternative perspectives, or simply expressing empathy or support. By doing so, you not only demonstrate that you are actively involved in the conversation, but also foster a sense of mutual respect and understanding. Appropriate responses can help steer the conversation in a meaningful direction, as they encourage the speaker to delve deeper into their ideas or experiences. This level of engagement allows for a more enriching and dynamic conversation, where both parties can learn and grow from each other's perspectives. It is important to note that nodding and responding appropriately should be done genuinely and authentically. Artificial or exaggerated nods and responses can be easily detected and may come across as insincere or disingenuous. It is essential to be attentive and responsive to the nuances of the conversation. This involves actively listening to what is being said, as well as paying attention to non-verbal cues such as tone of voice, facial expressions, and body language. By being fully present in the conversation, you can ensure that your nods and responses are appropriate and genuine. Nodding and responding appropriately may vary depending on cultural or social context. Certain gestures or verbal cues that are considered appropriate in one culture may be perceived differently in another. It is crucial to be mindful of these cultural differences and adapt your behavior accordingly. This can involve learning about the cultural norms and values of the individuals you are conversing with, as well as being sensitive and respectful of their perspectives. By doing so, you can foster a positive and inclusive environment for conversation, where diverse voices and ideas are welcomed and respected. Nodding and responding appropriately are key elements of being a good conversationalist. They demonstrate active listening, engagement, and understanding, and contribute to a meaningful and enriching conversation. It is important to be genuine and authentic in your nods and responses, as well as mindful of cultural differences. By embodying these qualities, you can create an atmosphere of mutual respect and understanding, and foster connections and meaningful dialogue with others.

ASKING RELEVANT QUESTIONS

Asking relevant questions is another important aspect of being a good conversationalist. When engaging in a conversation, it is crucial to actively listen and show genuine interest in the other person's thoughts and opinions. One effective way to do this is by asking relevant questions that prompt the speaker to elaborate further on their ideas. By asking thoughtful questions, we not only encourage the speaker to delve deeper into a topic, but we also demonstrate our engagement and willingness to understand their perspective. It is important to note that asking relevant questions goes beyond simply asking for clarification or seeking more information. It involves asking questions that foster meaningful discussions and allow the conversation to flow naturally. These questions should not be pre-rehearsed or generic, but rather tailored to the specific context and content of the conversation. By asking relevant questions, we signal to the speaker that we value their input and are actively seeking to learn from them. Asking relevant questions helps to keep the conversation balanced and prevents it from becoming one-sided. Instead of dominating the conversation with our own ideas and experiences, we give the other person an opportunity to express themselves fully, while also giving ourselves a chance to learn and grow from their insights. Asking relevant questions can also help to forge a stronger connection between the conversational partners. It shows that we are not only interested in the topic being discussed, but also in the person themselves. We are willing to invest our time and energy to understand their perspective and engage in a meaningful exchange of ideas. In this way, asking relevant questions creates a sense of mutual respect and fosters a more meaningful and memorable conversation. It is important to strike a balance when asking questions. While it is crucial to ask relevant and engaging questions, we should also be mindful of the flow of the conversation and avoid bombarding the speaker with an excessive number of inquiries. Asking too many questions can be overwhelming and may disrupt the natural rhythm of the conversation. Instead, it is important to be attentive to the speaker's cues and to ask questions strategically, at appropriate intervals. By doing so, we can ensure that the conversation remains fluid and enjoyable for both parties involved. Asking relevant questions is an essential skill for being a good conversationalist. It allows us to demonstrate our genuine interest, foster meaningful discussions, and forge stronger connections with others. By actively listening and tailoring our questions to the conversation at hand, we can create engaging and memorable interactions that enrich our lives and the lives of those with whom we converse.

In addition to actively listening and using open-ended questions, another important aspect of being a good conversationalist is expressing empathy and understanding. Empathy involves putting oneself in the shoes of the other person, trying to understand their perspective, and showing genuine concern for their feelings and emotions. When a conversationalist expresses empathy, it creates a safe and comfortable environment for the speaker to open up and share their thoughts and experiences. It also allows the listener to better connect with the speaker on a deeper level. One way to express empathy is through verbal cues such as saying phrases like "I understand", "That must have been really difficult", or "I can see why you feel that way". These responses show that the listener is actively engaged in the conversation and acknowledges the speaker's feelings. Using nonverbal cues such as nodding, maintaining eye contact, and using appropriate facial expressions are essential in expressing empathy. These nonverbal cues signal to the speaker that the listener is fully present and engaged in the conversation. A good conversationalist does not interrupt or invalidate the speaker's feelings. They let the speaker express themselves fully before interjecting with their own thoughts or experiences. This allows the speaker to feel heard and validated, which can strengthen the bond between the conversationalists. A good conversationalist avoids judgment or criticism when expressing empathy. They create an accepting and non-judgmental space where the speaker can freely express their thoughts and feelings without fear of being evaluated or criticized. This encourages open and honest conversations where both parties feel comfortable sharing their perspectives. It is important for a conversationalist to remember that expressing empathy does not mean they have to agree with everything the speaker says or condone their actions, but rather to validate their feelings and experiences. Being genuinely interested in the speaker and their topic of discussion is a crucial aspect of expressing empathy. It involves actively engaging in the conversation, asking follow-up questions, and showing curiosity about the speaker's thoughts and experiences. By displaying a genuine interest, the listener demonstrates that they value the speaker's opinions and are invested in the conversation. Expressing empathy and understanding is a vital skill in becoming a good conversationalist. It helps create a supportive and open environment where both parties feel valued and heard. By actively expressing empathy through verbal and non-verbal cues, avoiding judgment or criticism, and displaying genuine interest, a conversationalist can foster meaningful and enriching conversations.

III. NON-VERBAL COMMUNICATION

Non-verbal communication plays a critical role in effective conversation, often carrying more weight than spoken words. It encompasses various elements such as body language, facial expressions, gestures, and even eye contact. A skilled conversationalist understands the power of non-verbal cues and utilizes them strategically to enhance the message they want to convey. Firstly, body language can greatly influence the success of a conversation. By being aware of one's own body posture and making conscious efforts to maintain an open and engaged stance, a conversationalist can create a comfortable environment for all parties involved. For example, leaning slightly towards the speaker while nodding in agreement conveys active listening and interest. Crossing one's arms can signal defensiveness or disinterest, hindering the flow of communication. Mastering the art of body language is crucial for establishing rapport and fostering meaningful conversations.

Facial expressions, another component of non-verbal communication, can have a profound impact on the way a conversation is perceived. Smiling, for instance, can instantly create a warm and positive atmosphere. Maintaining eye contact while listening and speaking reflects attentiveness and respect, provoking a sense of trust between the conversational partners. Excessive blinking or avoiding eye contact might suggest dishonesty or unease, hindering effective communication. As a result, a skilled conversationalist understands the importance of managing facial expressions to convey the intended emotions and sentiments accurately. Gestures can also play a pivotal role in conversation, aiding in emphasizing points or clarifying intentions. For instance, using hand movements to illustrate a concept can make it more comprehensible and engaging for the listener. Excessive or inappropriate gestures can be distracting or even offensive, hindering effective communication. A conversationalist must strike a balance between using gestures to enhance the conversation and avoiding excessive or inappropriate movements. The appropriate use of personal space can significantly impact the dynamics of a conversation. While some cultures value close personal space, others prefer a more considerable distance between conversational partners. Understanding and respecting these cultural norms is essential to prevent any discomfort or misunderstandings during the conversation. A good conversationalist is aware of personal space preferences and adjusts accordingly, ensuring a harmonious and mutually respectful exchange of ideas. Non-verbal communication is a vital component of effective conversation, providing insights into emotions, intentions, and overall engagement. A skilled conversationalist understands how to utilize body language, facial expressions, gestures, and personal space to their advantage, creating an atmosphere of trust, openness, and attentiveness. By mastering the art of non-verbal cues, one can become a good conversationalist, fostering meaningful connections and enhancing the quality of interactions.

IMPORTANCE OF BODY LANGUAGE

One cannot underestimate the importance of body language in becoming a good conversationalist. While verbal communication is undoubtedly crucial, our nonverbal cues often speak louder than words themselves. Body language encompasses a vast array of gestures, facial expressions, and postures that can convey a multitude of emotions and messages. For instance, maintaining eye contact with the speaker demonstrates interest and attentiveness, while avoiding it may imply disinterest or distraction. Similarly, a friendly smile can instantly establish a welcoming and warm environment, making the other person feel comfortable and open to conversation. On the other hand, crossed arms or fidgeting may indicate defensiveness or discomfort, creating barriers to effective communication. Understanding how to interpret these nonverbal cues and consciously using them to our advantage can greatly enhance our conversational skills.

Body language can often provide valuable insights into a person's true intentions or feelings that may not be explicitly expressed through words alone. Through the observation of someone's gestures, posture, or facial expressions, we can gain a deeper understanding of their state of mind and emotional well-being. This knowledge allows us to respond with empathy and sensitivity, creating a supportive and compassionate environment for conversation. Being aware of our own body language enables us to regulate our emotional responses and present ourselves authentically. The impact of body language extends beyond individual interactions and plays a pivotal role in group dynamics. In group settings, body language can influence the overall tone and atmosphere of the conversation. A person who maintains an open and relaxed posture can encourage others to feel more at ease, leading to increased participation and collaboration. Conversely, a closed-off or confrontational stance can create tension and inhibit the flow of ideas. Thus, understanding and utilizing positive body language in group settings can foster a sense of unity and enable effective communication among members.

Mastering the art of body language is essential to becoming a good conversationalist. By paying attention to both our own nonverbal cues and those of others, we can establish rapport, convey our thoughts and emotions effectively, and foster meaningful connections. The ability to interpret body language allows us to empathize with others and create an inclusive conversational environment. Body language plays a crucial role in group dynamics, shaping the overall atmosphere and enabling effective communication among members. Incorporating body language skills into our conversational toolkit equips us with a powerful tool for creating successful and engaging interactions.

POSTURE AND GESTURES

One important aspect of good conversational skills is posture and gestures. Nonverbal communication plays a significant role in determining how effectively a conversation is received and understood. Posture refers to the way one carries oneself during a conversation, while gestures involve the movements and positioning of one's hands and body. Maintaining good posture during a conversation conveys confidence and attentiveness to the speaker. Sitting or standing up straight indicates that one is engaged and interested in the conversation, while slouching or hunching suggests disinterest or boredom. Maintaining eye contact with the speaker demonstrates respect and shows that one is actively listening. Avoiding excessive fidgeting or crossing of arms can also signal openness and receptiveness to the conversation. In addition to posture, gestures are also crucial in conveying meaning and enhancing communication. Hand gestures, when used appropriately, can emphasize key points and make the conversation more engaging. For example, using gestures to illustrate the size or shape of an object being discussed can help the listener visualize and better understand the topic. It is important to avoid excessive or distracting gestures, as they may detract from the conversation rather than enhance it. In addition to hand gestures, facial expressions also play a significant role in nonverbal communication. Smiling, for instance, can create a positive and welcoming atmosphere, encouraging the speaker to feel comfortable and confident in expressing their thoughts. Conversely, a frowning or indifferent expression may discourage the speaker from fully engaging in the conversation. Posture and gestures are essential components of effective conversation. They can convey a wide range of meanings and emotions, often more powerfully than words alone. Being mindful of one's posture and gestures demonstrates respect, engagement, and receptiveness, which are key attributes of a good conversationalist. By maintaining good posture, using appropriate gestures, and being aware of facial expressions, one can significantly enhance the quality and impact of their conversations. Nonverbal cues can also help in fostering a connection with the speaker and creating a more memorable and enjoyable conversation experience for both parties. Developing mastery in these aspects of nonverbal communication requires practice and self-awareness. Regularly observing and analyzing one's own posture and gesture habits, as well as seeking feedback from others, can aid in self-improvement. By consistently paying attention to these nonverbal cues, individuals can refine their conversational skills and become more effective communicators. Posture and gestures serve as the silent language that complements and enriches verbal communication, contributing to an overall successful and engaging conversation.

FACIAL EXPRESSIONS

Facial expressions play a crucial role in effective communication and are an important aspect of being a good conversationalist. Our faces can convey a wide range of emotions and sentiments, often without saying a word. Genuine and appropriate facial expressions can enhance the clarity and sincerity of verbal communication, making it easier for others to understand and connect with us. In conversation, facial expressions serve as visual cues that indicate our level of interest, attentiveness, and engagement. For example, maintaining eye contact and nodding appropriately can show the speaker that we are actively listening and engaged in the conversation. These nonverbal cues can also create a sense of trust and empathy, as they signal our willingness to understand and empathize with others. Facial expressions can help to clarify the intended meaning behind our words and prevent misunderstandings. For instance, a smile can indicate that we are expressing genuine happiness or agreement, whereas a furrowed brow might suggest confusion or disagreement. By aligning our facial expressions with our verbal communication, we can convey our true emotions and intentions, thereby enhancing the overall effectiveness of our conversations. It is important to note that not all facial expressions are universal, and their interpretation can vary across different cultures and contexts. The same expression may convey different meanings or emotions depending on the cultural background and social norms of the individuals involved. It is essential to be mindful of these cultural variations in facial expressions to ensure effective cross-cultural communication. It is important to consider individual differences in facial expressions. Some individuals may naturally have more animated and expressive faces, while others may be more stoic and reserved. It is crucial to respect these individual differences and not make assumptions or judgments based solely on someone's facial expressions.

In order to enhance our facial expressions in conversations, it can be helpful to practice self-awareness and emotional intelligence. Being aware of our own emotions and how they manifest on our faces can help us better understand and control our expressions. Being attuned to the emotions and expressions of others can enable us to adapt our own facial expressions to better match and respond to theirs. It is also valuable to pay attention to the feedback we receive from others regarding our facial expressions. If someone consistently misinterprets our expressions or finds them inappropriate, it may be worth reflecting on how we can adjust our expressions to be more congruent with our intended message. Facial expressions are a vital component of effective communication and being a good conversationalist. They provide visual cues that convey our emotions, attentiveness, and sincerity, thereby enhancing the overall clarity and connection in conversations. It is crucial to be aware of cultural variations and individual differences in facial expressions while also practicing self-awareness and emotional intelligence to ensure that our expressions align with our intended message. By honing our facial expressions, we can become more effective communicators and foster meaningful connections with others in our conversations.

MATCHING NON-VERBAL CUES WITH VERBAL COMMUNICATION

Matching non-verbal cues with verbal communication is essential to becoming a good conversationalist. Communication is a complex process that involves both verbal and non-verbal elements. While words are the primary means of conveying meaning, non-verbal cues, such as facial expressions, gestures, and body language, can greatly enhance or detract from the message being communicated. One key aspect of matching non-verbal cues with verbal communication is aligning one's facial expressions with the spoken words. When engaged in a conversation, individuals must be mindful of their expressions, as any incongruence between the verbal and non-verbal cues can lead to confusion or misinterpretation. For example, if someone is delivering good news but wearing a frown, the recipient may not fully believe or understand the positive message. On the other hand, matching a smile with happy words can reinforce the message and create a positive and engaging atmosphere. Similarly, it is crucial to synchronize one's gestures with the spoken words. Gestures can emphasize or reinforce certain points, making them more memorable or impactful. Gestures that contradict or distract from the verbal message can undermine effective communication. For instance, if someone is speaking about the importance of honesty while nervously fidgeting or averting their gaze, this can send mixed signals and diminish the credibility of their words. On the contrary, a strong and confident posture with appropriate hand gestures can enhance the speaker's credibility and make their message more convincing. Body language plays a crucial role in non-verbal communication. Matching one's body language to the content of the conversation can signal interest, engagement, and understanding. For instance, leaning in slightly towards the speaker can demonstrate attentiveness and signal that one is fully present in the conversation. On the other hand, crossing one's arms or leaning away can convey disinterest or defensiveness, hindering the flow of communication. Mirroring the other person's body language can also establish rapport and a sense of connection. Adopting similar postures and gestures can create a subconscious bond between individuals and foster a more comfortable and open atmosphere for conversation. A good conversationalist should pay attention to the non-verbal cues of their interlocutors. These cues can provide valuable insights into the underlying emotions, attitudes, or reactions of the other person. By being observant of facial expressions, body language, and tone of voice, one can customize their communication style to better connect with and understand the other person. For example, if someone appears tense or uncomfortable, adjusting one's approach by speaking in a soothing tone or displaying empathy through facial expressions can help alleviate their discomfort and create a more conducive environment for conversation. The effective matching of non-verbal cues with verbal communication is integral to becoming a good conversationalist. By aligning facial expressions, gestures, and body language with the spoken words, individuals can enhance their message, establish rapport, and promote effective communication. Attention to both one's own non-verbal cues and those of the other person can facilitate a more meaningful and satisfying conversation.

EXPRESSING EMPATHY THROUGH BODY LANGUAGE

Expressing empathy through body language is a vital component of being a good conversationalist. It involves using nonverbal cues to show understanding, support, and compassion towards the speaker. One powerful way to convey empathy through body language is by employing active listening skills. This includes maintaining eye contact with the speaker, nodding occasionally to indicate engagement, and maintaining an open and relaxed posture. These simple gestures can make the speaker feel heard and valued, fostering a deeper sense of connection and trust between both parties. Mirroring the speaker's body language can be another effective way to express empathy. By subtly imitating their gestures, facial expressions, and tone, the listener conveys a sense of being in sync with the speaker's emotions and experiences. This mirroring behavior can help create a sense of shared understanding and empathy, making the speaker feel more comfortable and supported. The use of appropriate facial expressions plays a crucial role in expressing empathy through body language. Facial expressions that reflect sadness, concern, or happiness depending on the situation can demonstrate that the listener genuinely cares about the speaker's emotions and experiences. A warm smile, a sympathetic frown, or a gentle touch on the shoulder can go a long way in conveying empathy and understanding to the speaker. The use of appropriate touch can also communicate empathy effectively. A comforting pat on the back or a gentle squeeze of the hand can provide reassurance and support to someone going through a difficult time. It is essential to be cautious when using touch as it can be interpreted differently by individuals and may violate personal boundaries. It is important to gauge the speaker's comfort level and proceed accordingly. Active mirroring of vocal cues and tone can significantly enhance the expression of empathy through body language. Matching the speaker's tone and pace of speech can make them feel heard and validated. By adopting a similar vocal cadence, pitch, and volume, the listener conveys an understanding of the speaker's emotional state, and it reinforces the connection between them. It is crucial to be authentic and natural in mirroring these vocal cues, as being too overt or insincere can have the opposite effect and diminish the sense of empathy. Empathy expressed through body language is a critical aspect of being a good conversationalist. By actively listening, mirroring the speaker's body language, utilizing appropriate facial expressions and touch, and matching vocal cues, a person can show genuine empathy and support to the speaker. By doing so, they create a safe and nurturing space for open communication and connection. Cultivating these skills can not only improve personal relationships but also professional interactions, fostering a positive and empathetic environment in all areas of life.

CONVEYING SINCERITY AND CONFIDENCE

A crucial aspect of being a good conversationalist is the ability to convey sincerity and confidence. Sincerity is essential in building trust and establishing a genuine connection with others. It involves being authentic, honest, and open in our interactions. When we express ourselves sincerely, we are able to communicate our true thoughts and emotions without pretense. This conveys a sense of vulnerability and creates an environment where others feel comfortable doing the same. Confidence, on the other hand, allows us to be assertive and self-assured in our conversations. It reflects our belief in ourselves and our ability to contribute meaningfully to the discussion. Confidence is not about being arrogant or dominating the conversation but rather about having a firm grasp of our thoughts and ideas. When we speak with confidence, we are more likely to command attention and engage others in a thoughtful exchange of ideas. Both sincerity and confidence are closely linked, as they require self-awareness and self-assurance. Understanding our own values, beliefs, and emotions is crucial for communicating sincerely and confidently. Without a strong sense of self, our words may lack conviction and come across as superficial or insincere. Conversely, a deep understanding of ourselves allows us to convey our thoughts and feelings genuinely, which facilitates meaningful connections with others. Being sincere and confident in our conversations also involves active listening. By actively listening to others, we show respect and genuine interest in their thoughts and perspectives. This not only enhances the quality of the conversation but also demonstrates our sincerity in seeking to understand others. Active listening ensures that we respond appropriately and effectively, conveying our thoughts with confidence while acknowledging and incorporating the ideas of others. It is also important to strike a balance between being sincere and confident without overpowering or disregarding the contributions of others. A good conversationalist understands the value of collaboration and respects the opinions of others, even when they differ from their own. They know how to express themselves sincerely and confidently while remaining open to new ideas and perspectives. Conveying sincerity and confidence is a vital skill for being a good conversationalist. Sincerity allows us to build trust and establish genuine connections with others, while confidence enables us to contribute assertively and self-assuredly to the conversation. The combination of sincerity and confidence creates an environment where meaningful and engaging discussions can take place. By practicing active listening and respecting the contributions of others, we can strike a balance between expressing ourselves sincerely and confidently, and fostering a collaborative and respectful conversation.

Good conversationalists understand the importance of being present in the moment. In today's fast-paced society, many people are constantly distracted by their devices, multitasking, or simply not fully engaged in the conversation. To be a good conversationalist, one must learn to give their undivided attention to the person they are conversing with. This means actively listening and responding in a meaningful way. Being present in the conversation allows for a deeper connection and understanding between individuals. It shows respect and signals to the speaker that their thoughts and opinions are valued. Giving someone your undivided attention can create a safe and comfortable environment, encouraging the speaker to open up and share more. When you are fully present, you are able to pick up on cues in the conversation, such as body language and tone of voice, which can provide deeper insight into the speaker's emotions and thoughts. By being aware of these cues, good conversationalists are able to respond appropriately, demonstrating empathy and understanding. This, in turn, fosters a sense of trust and rapport between the individuals. Another characteristic of a good conversationalist is the ability to ask thoughtful questions. Asking open-ended questions not only keeps the conversation flowing but also allows for more in-depth discussion. Good conversationalists understand the power of well-crafted questions to elicit thoughtful responses and to delve into the deeper layers of a topic or issue. These questions encourage the speaker to think critically and reflect on their own thoughts and ideas. Asking questions shows genuine interest in the speaker and their perspective. It demonstrates that you value their insights and are invested in the conversation. Good conversationalists are skilled at balancing the conversation, ensuring that it is not one-sided. They give the speaker the opportunity to express themselves fully while also contributing their own thoughts and ideas. This balance creates a dynamic and engaging conversation that is enjoyable for both parties. Good conversationalists are adaptable. They understand that every conversation is unique and requires different approaches. They are flexible in their communication style and able to tailor their approach to the individual they are conversing with. This adaptability allows for better communication and understanding. It also demonstrates respect for the other person's communication preferences. Good conversationalists are skilled at reading the room and adapting their tone, language, and style to fit the context. They know when to be formal or informal, serious or lighthearted, depending on the situation. This adaptability can help to create a comfortable and harmonious atmosphere, where both parties feel at ease expressing themselves openly. Being a good conversationalist requires being present, asking thoughtful questions, and being adaptable in communication style. These skills are not only beneficial in creating meaningful connections and relationships but are also essential for effective communication in various contexts. By actively practicing and developing these skills, one can become a better conversationalist and, consequently, enhance their interactions and relationships with others.

IV. SHOWING EMPATHY

Empathy is an essential aspect of being a good conversationalist. It involves the ability to understand and share the feelings of another person. Showing empathy allows individuals to connect on a deeper level by acknowledging the emotions and experiences of others. There are several ways to demonstrate empathy during a conversation. Firstly, active listening is crucial. By fully engaging with the speaker and giving them your undivided attention, you are showing that their words and emotions are valued. This can be achieved through maintaining eye contact, nodding in agreement, and providing verbal cues such as "I understand", or "That must have been tough". Secondly, paraphrasing and summarizing what the speaker has said can help to clarify their thoughts and feelings, indicating that you are actively trying to comprehend their perspective. This technique also presents an opportunity for the speaker to correct any misunderstandings and expand on their points. Thirdly, acknowledging and validating the emotions expressed by the speaker is a key component of empathy. This involves recognizing their feelings and responding in a supportive and non-judgmental manner. For example, if someone shares a personal struggle, acknowledging the difficulty of their situation and expressing compassion can create an environment of trust and understanding. Offering words of encouragement and reassurance can assure the speaker that their emotions are valid and that they are being heard. Avoiding judgment and refraining from imposing personal opinions or experiences is crucial in demonstrating empathy. It is essential to remember that every individual's experiences and emotions are unique, and imposing our own beliefs or experiences can invalidate their feelings. Instead, focusing on the speaker's perspective and being open-minded can foster connection and allow for a more genuine conversation.

Showing empathy not only benefits the person we are conversing with but also enhances our own communication skills and relationships. By demonstrating empathy, we create a safe environment for individuals to open up and share their thoughts and emotions freely. This can lead to deeper, more meaningful conversations, as it allows for a genuine exchange of ideas and experiences. Engaging in empathetic conversations can help us broaden our own perspectives and develop a greater sense of understanding and empathy towards others. In a world that often emphasizes individualism and self-interest, showing empathy serves as a powerful tool to bridge gaps and foster connections in our interpersonal relationships.

Empathy is a fundamental aspect of being a good conversationalist. By actively listening, paraphrasing, validating emotions, and avoiding judgment, we can demonstrate empathy and create a space for individuals to feel heard and understood. Cultivating empathy in our conversations not only benefits the person we are conversing with but also enhances our own communication skills and relationships. In a society that often lacks genuine connection, showing empathy is a powerful tool to create meaningful and authentic relationships. Let us strive to be empathetic conversationalists and foster connection and understanding in our interactions with others.

UNDERSTANDING THE SPEAKER'S PERSPECTIVE

Understanding the speaker's perspective is a crucial aspect of becoming a good conversationalist. It requires actively listening and acknowledging the speaker's thoughts and emotions. By doing so, one can gain a deeper understanding of their viewpoint and effectively engage in meaningful conversations. One way to understand the speaker's perspective is by practicing empathy, which entails putting oneself in the speaker's shoes and trying to see the situation from their point of view. This can be achieved by attentively listening to the speaker's words, tone of voice, and body language. Reflecting on one's personal experiences and emotions can help develop empathy towards the speaker. Another method to understand the speaker's perspective is to ask thoughtful and open-ended questions. By asking questions that allow the speaker to elaborate on their thoughts or feelings, one can gain further insight into their perspective. This not only demonstrates genuine interest in the conversation but also encourages the speaker to delve deeper into their opinions and experiences. Paraphrasing the speaker's words can be an effective way to understand their perspective. By restating the speaker's ideas or feelings in one's own words, it not only helps clarify their viewpoint but also shows that one is actively engaged in the conversation. Paraphrasing provides an opportunity for the speaker to confirm or clarify their intended meaning. It is important for a good conversationalist to avoid making assumptions about the speaker's perspective. Instead, suspending judgment and actively seeking to understand their viewpoint can lead to more meaningful conversations. Acknowledging and validating the speaker's emotions is another crucial aspect of understanding their perspective. Emotions play a significant role in shaping one's perspective, and by recognizing and validating the speaker's emotions, one can establish a deeper level of connection and trust. This can be done through supportive statements or affirmations that show empathy and understanding, such as "I can understand why you might feel that way". It is also important to be aware of one's own biases and prejudices that may hinder the understanding of the speaker's perspective. By recognizing and challenging these biases, a good conversationalist can ensure that they are approaching the conversation with an open mind. Understanding the speaker's perspective is essential in becoming a good conversationalist. It requires active listening, empathy, asking thoughtful questions, paraphrasing, avoiding assumptions, acknowledging emotions, and challenging one's biases. By practicing these techniques, one can foster meaningful conversations and develop a deeper understanding and appreciation for others' viewpoints. This ability to understand and connect with others will not only enhance one's conversational skills but also promote empathy and create more inclusive and understanding communities.

PRACTICING ACTIVE EMPATHY

Active empathy is the ability to fully understand and share the feelings of another person, and to respond in a way that acknowledges and validates those emotions. This requires being present in the moment, giving the speaker our full attention, and making a genuine effort to see things from their perspective. By practicing active empathy, we create a safe and supportive space for the speaker to express themselves freely, which in turn fosters a deeper and more meaningful conversation.

One way to practice active empathy is by practicing active listening. Active listening involves not only hearing the words that someone is saying, but also paying attention to their tone, body language, and non-verbal cues. By doing so, we can gain a better understanding of the emotions behind their words, and respond in a way that shows we truly understand and care about what they are saying. This can be as simple as nodding or making encouraging gestures, or asking probing questions to prompt further elaboration. By actively listening, we show the speaker that we are fully engaged in the conversation and value their perspective. Another important aspect of active empathy is being able to put ourselves in the other person's shoes. This requires setting aside our own biases and preconceived notions, and truly trying to see the world from their point of view. By doing so, we can better understand their experiences, beliefs, and values, which allows us to have a more empathetic and open-minded conversation. This does not mean that we have to agree with everything the other person says, but rather that we are willing to consider their perspective and approach the conversation with an open mind. In addition to active listening and perspective-taking, active empathy also involves responding in a way that validates the speaker's emotions. This can be done through supportive statements such as "I can see why you feel that way" or "That must have been really difficult for you". By acknowledging and validating the speaker's emotions, we create an environment where they feel heard and understood, which encourages further conversation and connection.

Practicing active empathy not only benefits the conversation itself, but also strengthens our overall ability to connect and relate to others. By cultivating empathy, we become more attuned to the emotions and needs of those around us, leading to more fulfilling and meaningful relationships. Empathy allows us to navigate conflicts and disagreements with greater understanding and compassion. Practicing active empathy is a fundamental skill for becoming a good conversationalist. By actively listening, putting ourselves in the other person's shoes, and responding in a validating and supportive way, we create an atmosphere of understanding and connection. This not only enhances the conversation itself, but also strengthens our ability to relate and connect with others on a deeper level.

AVOIDING JUDGMENTAL ATTITUDES

In addition to maintaining a positive mindset and being an active listener, another essential element of being a good conversationalist is avoiding judgmental attitudes. It is crucial to recognize the importance of accepting others without passing judgment on their beliefs, opinions, or experiences. Judgmental attitudes can often hinder the development of meaningful conversations and may create an uncomfortable atmosphere for both parties involved. When engaging in conversation, it is inevitable that individuals will encounter perspectives that differ from their own. It is essential to approach these differences with an open mind and a willingness to learn from others. By refraining from judgment, conversation participants can foster an environment of respect and understanding. Judgmental attitudes can perpetuate stereotypes and reinforce prejudices, ultimately hindering personal growth and hindering the establishment of genuine connections with others. Avoiding judgmental attitudes requires self-awareness and empathy. It is vital to understand that everyone has unique experiences and perspectives shaped by their backgrounds and individual journeys. When engaging in conversation, it is important to remind oneself that there is no universal right or wrong perspective. Instead, each individual's viewpoint should be valued and respected. By embracing such a mindset, one can actively avoid making quick assumptions or passing unnecessary judgments. For instance, instead of fixating on someone's choice of beliefs or opinions, one should focus on understanding their reasons and experiences that led them to conjure such notions. Such an approach promotes open dialogues and encourages the exchange of diverse ideas and perspectives. Avoiding judgmental attitudes allows individuals to create a welcoming and inclusive atmosphere that encourages authentic sharing. When conversation participants feel accepted and validated, they are more likely to express themselves honestly, leading to deeper and more meaningful discussions. By showing respect for the thoughts and experiences of others, individuals can establish strong connections and form lasting bonds with those around them. Embracing non-judgmental attitudes can foster personal growth by exposing individuals to unique perspectives and challenging their own beliefs and assumptions.

It is important to note that avoiding judgmental attitudes does not mean abandoning personal values or compromising one's principles. Engaging in conversation does not require one to agree with every viewpoint expressed; rather, it involves acknowledging and respecting differences while remaining open to the possibility of broadening one's understanding. It is important to approach discussions with curiosity and a genuine desire to comprehend alternative perspectives, maintaining an open mind without compromising one's own values. Avoiding judgmental attitudes plays a crucial role in becoming a proficient conversationalist. By recognizing and respecting the diversity of beliefs and opinions, individuals can maintain an inclusive environment conducive to rich and meaningful dialogue. Approaching discussions with empathy and a willingness to learn from others allows for personal growth and the establishment of genuine connections. By avoiding judgment, one can pave the way for productive and impactful conversations with individuals from all walks of life.

OFFERING EMOTIONAL SUPPORT

People often seek solace in conversation when they are going through difficult times or facing challenges. By providing emotional support, one can create a sense of empathy, understanding, and connection. This entails actively listening and demonstrating genuine concern for the other person's emotions. Empathy requires putting oneself in the other person's shoes, recognizing their feelings, and validating their experiences. One way to offer emotional support is by using verbal and nonverbal cues that indicate understanding and validation, such as nodding, making eye contact, and providing verbal affirmations like "I understand" or "That sounds really tough". Using open-ended questions can help encourage the other person to express their emotions more freely. For example, asking "How does that make you feel?" or "What has been going through your mind?" allows the person to delve deeper into their emotions and share more openly. It is important to remember that emotional support does not entail offering unsolicited advice or attempting to fix the other person's problems. Instead, it involves creating a safe and non-judgmental space for them to share and express themselves. Silence can also be a powerful tool in offering emotional support, as it allows the other person to gather their thoughts, process their emotions, and feel heard. Mirroring the other person's emotions and providing validation can also contribute to a supportive conversation. By reflecting their feelings back to them, such as saying "That must have been really frustrating" or "I can see why you feel that way", one can show that their emotions are acknowledged and understood. Offering emotional support may also involve expressing empathy through one's own personal experiences, if relevant. Sharing a similar struggle or recounting a challenging time can help the other person feel less alone and provide a sense of solidarity. Being mindful of one's own emotions and vulnerabilities is crucial in this aspect, as it ensures that the focus remains on the other person's emotions and needs. Offering emotional support is a fundamental component of being a good conversationalist. It requires active listening, empathy, validation, and creating a safe space for someone to share their emotions. By providing emotional support, conversationalists can help alleviate the burdens of others, foster understanding and empathy, and build deeper connections. In an increasingly fast-paced and disconnected world, offering emotional support can truly make a difference in someone's life.

ACKNOWLEDGING THE SPEAKER'S FEELINGS

In addition to actively listening and practicing empathy, being a good conversationalist also requires acknowledging the speaker's feelings. This aspect of effective communication is crucial in fostering a supportive and understanding environment. When engaging in a conversation, it is important to recognize and validate the emotions expressed by the speaker. This can be done through non-verbal cues such as nodding, making appropriate facial expressions, or maintaining eye contact. Verbal affirmations such as "I understand how you feel" or "That sounds really challenging" can assure the speaker that their emotions are being acknowledged and respected. By acknowledging the speaker's feelings, we demonstrate our empathy and create a safe space for them to express themselves fully.

Acknowledging the speaker's feelings is not only about providing reassurance, but it also helps to deepen the connection and foster trust within the conversation. When individuals feel that their emotions are being acknowledged and understood, they are more likely to open up and share their thoughts and experiences more honestly. This level of vulnerability can lead to more meaningful conversations and can help to establish stronger relationships. By validating someone's feelings, we show them that we care about their emotional well-being and are invested in their experiences. It is essential, To acknowledge the speaker's feelings genuinely and authentically. Simply going through the motions of nodding or saying formulaic phrases without actually empathizing with the speaker's emotions can be detrimental to the conversation. To genuinely acknowledge someone's feelings, we must make a conscious effort to put ourselves in their shoes and try to understand their perspective. This involves being present in the moment and actively listening to their words, tone, and body language. By being fully engaged in the conversation, we can respond in a more meaningful and empathetic way. Acknowledging the speaker's feelings is a crucial aspect of being a good conversationalist. By validating and demonstrating empathy towards the emotions expressed by the speaker, we create a supportive and understanding environment. This not only helps to foster trust and deepen connections within conversations but also shows that we genuinely care about someone's emotional well-being. It is important to practice active and authentic listening, making conscious efforts to understand the speaker's perspective. By doing so, we create a safe space for individuals to express themselves fully and contribute to more meaningful conversations.

PROVIDING VALIDATION AND ENCOURAGEMENT

Another important aspect of being a good conversationalist is providing validation and encouragement to the other person. People naturally seek validation for their thoughts, opinions, and experiences, and oftentimes, they engage in conversations as a means of seeking this validation. As a good conversationalist, it is crucial to acknowledge and validate the other person's feelings and experiences, even if they differ from our own. This can be done by actively listening to what the person is saying, making eye contact, nodding or using other nonverbal cues to show that we are engaged in the conversation. By providing validation, we make the other person feel heard and understood, creating a safe and comfortable environment for them to express themselves. Offering encouragement is essential in fostering a positive and constructive conversation. Encouragement can come in many forms – it can be a simple compliment, a word of praise, or expressing interest in the other person's ideas. By offering encouragement, we boost the other person's confidence and self-esteem, which in turn enhances their willingness to share more and engage in an open and productive dialogue. Encouragement can help motivate the other person to express their thoughts and feelings more freely, allowing for a deeper and more meaningful conversation. It is important to note that validation and encouragement should be genuine and sincere. Empty compliments or insincere praise can be easily detected and may come across as disingenuous or manipulative, thus undermining the trust and authenticity of the conversation. It is crucial to be mindful of our words and actions and ensure that our validation and encouragement are genuine and from the heart. Providing validation and encouragement is not only beneficial for the other person, but it can also enrich our own conversational experiences. By actively listening and validating others, we enhance our empathetic skills and broaden our perspectives. We gain a deeper understanding of different viewpoints and develop the ability to see beyond our own biases and preconceptions. This not only promotes personal growth but also facilitates mutual respect and understanding among individuals. Being a good conversationalist involves providing validation and encouragement to the other person. By actively listening, acknowledging their thoughts and experiences, and offering genuine validation, we create a safe and comfortable environment for them to express themselves. By providing encouragement, we boost their confidence, motivation, and self-esteem, fostering a positive and constructive conversation. The act of validating and encouraging others not only benefits them but also enriches our own conversational experiences, allowing for a deeper understanding and connection with others.

In addition to actively listening and asking open-ended questions, another important aspect of being a good conversationalist is having the ability to empathize with others. Empathy is the ability to understand and share the feelings of another person. When engaging in a conversation, it is important to be able to put yourself in the shoes of the other person and try to understand their perspective. By doing so, you can create a deeper connection and make the other person feel valued and heard. Empathy allows us to be more sensitive to the needs and emotions of others. It is a key component of building trust and maintaining healthy relationships. In order to develop empathy, it is crucial to practice active listening skills. Instead of simply waiting for our turn to speak, we should focus on truly understanding the other person's point of view. We can do this by paying attention to their body language, facial expressions, and tone of voice. These nonverbal cues can often reveal more about a person's emotions than their words alone. By tuning into these signals, we can gain a better understanding of what the person is experiencing and feeling. It is important to be mindful of our own biases and assumptions. We all have our own unique experiences and perspectives that shape the way we interpret the world. It is important to recognize that others may have different viewpoints and experiences, and to approach conversations with an open mind. Having empathy also involves the ability to validate and acknowledge the emotions of others. We should strive to make others feel heard and understood by acknowledging their feelings and experiences, even if we may not agree with them. This can be done by using phrases such as "I understand how you feel" or "That must have been really difficult for you". By offering this validation, we can create a safe space for open and honest communication. It is important to remember that empathy is not just limited to words. Small gestures such as a nod of the head, a smile, or a touch on the arm can go a long way in showing that we care and are actively engaged in the conversation. These simple acts of empathy can help to establish rapport and build meaningful connections with others. Being a good conversationalist involves the ability to empathize with others. By actively listening, seeking to understand others' perspectives, validating emotions, and using nonverbal cues, we can develop empathy and create more meaningful and fulfilling conversations.

V. DEVELOPING EMOTIONAL INTELLIGENCE

Developing emotional intelligence is a crucial aspect of becoming a good conversationalist. Emotional intelligence refers to the ability to recognize and manage one's own emotions, as well as effectively understand and respond to the emotions of others. It involves empathy, self-awareness, and the ability to regulate one's emotions in social interactions. When it comes to conversations, emotional intelligence allows individuals to connect with others on a deeper level, facilitating meaningful and satisfying interactions. To develop emotional intelligence, one must first cultivate self-awareness. It is important to have insight into one's own emotions, thoughts, and reactions in order to better understand how these factors influence conversations. By recognizing their own emotional triggers and patterns, individuals can develop strategies to manage their emotions in a more constructive way during conversations. This self-awareness also allows individuals to be more genuine and authentic in their interactions, as they are able to express their emotions honestly and appropriately. Empathy plays a crucial role in developing emotional intelligence. Empathy involves the ability to understand and share the feelings of others, allowing individuals to connect with people on a deeper level. In conversations, being empathetic means actively listening to others, paying attention to their non-verbal cues, and responding in a way that validates their emotions and experiences. By empathizing with others, individuals can create a safe and supportive environment, fostering trust and openness in conversations.

In addition to self-awareness and empathy, regulating emotions is another important aspect of emotional intelligence. In conversations, individuals may encounter situations or topics that elicit strong emotional reactions. Developing the ability to regulate these emotions, rather than letting them dictate the course of the conversation, is crucial to maintaining effective communication. This involves recognizing when emotions are starting to escalate and actively choosing how to respond in a calm and rational manner. By expressing emotions in a controlled and constructive way, individuals can prevent conflicts and misunderstandings from arising during conversations.

Developing emotional intelligence also involves being mindful of the cultural and social contexts in which conversations take place. Different cultures and social groups may have varying norms and expectations regarding emotional expression and communication styles. Understanding and respecting these differences can greatly enhance one's ability to engage in meaningful conversations with individuals from diverse backgrounds. By being mindful of cultural sensitivities and adapting one's communication style accordingly, individuals can foster inclusivity and create an environment in which everyone feels valued and heard. Developing emotional intelligence is an important aspect of becoming a good conversationalist. It involves cultivating self-awareness, empathy, and the ability to regulate one's emotions in social interactions. By developing these skills, individuals can connect with others on a deeper level, create an open and supportive environment, and navigate conversations more effectively. Emotional intelligence enables individuals to

have more meaningful and satisfying interactions, contributing
to their personal growth and enhancing their relationships with
others.

SELF-AWARENESS IN CONVERSATIONS

Being self-aware means being fully present in the conversation and understanding one's own thoughts, feelings, and actions in the context of the interaction. It involves recognizing and managing one's emotions, listening actively, and adapting one's communication style to the needs of the other person. Self-awareness also includes recognizing and responding appropriately to nonverbal cues such as body language and facial expressions. By being self-aware, a conversationalist can ensure that their words and actions align with their intended message and that they are able to effectively contribute to the conversation. Self-awareness allows individuals to monitor their own behavior and make adjustments if they notice negative patterns or habits that may hinder effective communication.

In order to develop self-awareness in conversations, it is important to start by cultivating Mindfulness. Mindfulness involves paying attention to the present moment without judgment and being fully aware of one's thoughts, feelings, and bodily sensations. By practicing Mindfulness regularly, individuals can develop a greater sense of self-awareness, which can then be applied to conversations. Mindfulness can also help individuals notice any distractions or internal thoughts that may be interfering with their ability to be fully present in the conversation.

Active listening is another crucial aspect of self-awareness in conversations. This involves not only hearing the words being said but also fully comprehending and understanding the meaning behind them. Active listening requires giving the speaker one's full attention, which can be achieved by maintaining eye contact, nodding or using other nonverbal cues to show engagement, and refraining from interrupting or bringing the conversation back to oneself. By actively listening, individuals can demonstrate respect and empathy towards the speaker and show that they value their perspectives and experiences.

Self-awareness in conversations involves being adaptable and flexible in one's communication style. This entails recognizing the needs and preferences of the other person and adjusting one's behavior accordingly. For example, if the other person seems reserved or shy, it may be necessary to ask open-ended questions or provide encouragement to elicit their participation. Adapting one's communication style can also involve being aware of one's own biases or assumptions and making an effort to approach the conversation without preconceived notions. By being open-minded and receptive to different perspectives, individuals can create a more inclusive and enriching conversational environment. Self-awareness in conversations is a vital skill for becoming a good conversationalist.

It involves being fully present, mindful, and attentive to one's own thoughts, feelings, and actions. Self-awareness also involves actively listening to the speaker, showing respect and empathy, and being adaptable in one's communication style. By cultivating self-awareness, individuals can enhance their ability to communicate effectively, establish meaningful connections with others, and contribute to more engaging and fulfilling conversations.

RECOGNIZING PERSONAL BIASES

Although often overlooked, recognizing personal biases is a crucial aspect of becoming a good conversationalist. Each individual holds a unique set of beliefs, values, and experiences that shape their perspective on the world. These biases can heavily influence our thoughts, opinions, and interactions with others. Recognizing personal biases is essential in engaging in meaningful conversations, as it allows individuals to be aware of the potential impact their biases may have on the dialogue. Acknowledging these biases can help individuals approach conversations with an open and receptive mindset, fostering a more inclusive and respectful exchange of ideas. By actively seeking to identify and understand our own biases, we can begin to challenge and expand our perspectives, enabling us to engage in conversations that are more balanced and objective.

The first step in recognizing personal biases is having an awareness of their existence. We all have biases, whether we are conscious of them or not. These biases can stem from various sources, including our culture, upbringing, education, and even social media exposure. By being honest with ourselves and accepting that we carry biases, we can begin to examine the role they play in our thoughts and actions. Self-reflection is key in this process, as it allows us to evaluate our beliefs and values critically. Recognizing personal biases involves actively listening and empathizing with others. Engaging in conversations requires us to suspend judgment and truly listen to what others are saying. This allows us to better understand their perspectives and experiences, even if they differ from our own. By putting ourselves in others' shoes, we can gain insight into the potential biases we might hold and the impact they can have on how we interpret information and communicate our own views.

Being open to feedback is also instrumental in recognizing personal biases. It can be uncomfortable to have our biases challenged, but it is an essential part of personal growth and becoming a good conversationalist. Constructive criticism allows us to see where our blind spots may lie and provides an opportunity for self-improvement. When someone points out a bias we may have, it is important to reflect on their feedback rather than becoming defensive. This willingness to learn and adapt is key to fostering productive and inclusive conversations.

Recognizing personal biases is not only crucial for personal growth, but also for becoming a good conversationalist. Through self-reflection, active listening, and openness to feedback, individuals can uncover and challenge their biases, leading to more objective and inclusive conversations. By understanding the potential impact our biases have on our thoughts and interactions, we can foster an environment where diverse viewpoints are respected and valued. Becoming aware of personal biases is an ongoing process, but it is an essential step towards becoming a more engaging and effective communicator.

MANAGING EMOTIONAL REACTIONS

Managing emotional reactions is a crucial skill in becoming a good conversationalist. When engaging in conversation, it is inevitable that we may encounter differing opinions or opposing viewpoints that can elicit strong emotional reactions. Allowing these emotions to control our behavior can be detrimental to the conversation and hinder any chance of productive dialogue. One important aspect of managing emotional reactions is self-awareness. By being aware of our own emotions and understanding what triggers these reactions, we are better equipped to control and regulate them during a conversation. This enables us to respond more thoughtfully and rationally, rather than reacting impulsively based on our emotions. Active listening plays a vital role in managing emotional reactions. By fully listening to the words and perspectives of others, we can gain a deeper understanding of their viewpoint and the reasons behind their emotions. This empathetic approach can help defuse potential conflicts and create an environment of mutual respect. Managing emotional reactions involves practicing patience and tolerance. It is essential to remind ourselves that everyone is entitled to their own opinions and emotions, even if they differ from ours. Instead of becoming defensive or aggressive, we should strive to be understanding and open-minded. By demonstrating patience, we allow others the space to express themselves fully, fostering a more constructive conversation and potentially finding common ground. Reframing our mindset can be a valuable tool in managing emotional reactions. Rather than approaching a conversation with the objective of winning an argument, we should aim to foster understanding and find a resolution. This shift in perspective can help to dissipate any negative emotions and create a more collaborative and productive atmosphere. Managing emotional reactions requires the ability to assert oneself effectively. Instead of reacting emotionally, one should strive to communicate assertively, expressing their thoughts and emotions in an honest and respectful manner. Assertive communication allows us to convey our perspective clearly, without aggressiveness or passiveness, and encourages others to reciprocate in kind. Managing emotional reactions involves recognizing the limits of a conversation. Not every discussion will lead to an agreement or a change in someone's opinion or emotions, and it is important to accept this reality. In such cases, it is crucial to know when to disengage and respect the boundaries of the conversation. Accepting differing perspectives and allowing others to hold onto their emotions without judgment can contribute to maintaining good rapport and avoiding unnecessary conflicts. Managing emotional reactions is a fundamental aspect of becoming a good conversationalist. By cultivating self-awareness, actively listening, practicing patience, reframing our mindset, employing assertive communication, and recognizing the limits of a conversation, we can navigate intricate conversations effectively. Such a skill set leads to more constructive discussions, fosters understanding, and promotes positive relationships in both personal and professional settings.

RECOGNIZING AND UNDERSTANDING OTHERS' EMOTIONS

By paying close attention to nonverbal cues and verbal expressions, one can gain valuable insights into the emotions being experienced by the person they are conversing with. This skill is particularly important in establishing rapport and building meaningful connections with others. When we are able to accurately recognize and understand someone's emotions, we can respond in a way that is empathetic and supportive, creating a safe and comfortable environment for further conversation. This ability to be emotionally attuned and responsive can significantly enhance the quality of our interactions.

One way to recognize others' emotions is through the observation of nonverbal cues such as facial expressions, body language, and tone of voice. These cues often provide crucial information about how the individual is feeling, even when their words may not explicitly express these emotions. For instance, a furrowed brow, clenched fists, or crossed arms may indicate signs of frustration or anger, while a smile and relaxed posture may signify happiness or contentment. By actively paying attention to these nonverbal signals, we can better understand the underlying emotions that may be influencing the conversation, allowing us to respond appropriately and with empathy.

Being able to recognize and understand others' emotions requires active listening and attentiveness. This means giving the person our full focus, avoiding distractions and truly engaging with what they are saying. By listening attentively, we can pick up on subtle vocal nuances, such as changes in pitch or volume, that can provide valuable insights into the speaker's emotional state. By paying close attention to the content of their words, we can gain a deeper understanding of their thoughts and feelings. This active listening serves as a foundation for responding empathetically and respectfully, creating a space for open and meaningful dialogue. Understanding others' emotions also involves empathy, which requires putting ourselves in the other person's shoes and trying to experience their feelings as if they were our own. By adopting this perspective, we can develop a genuine sense of care and concern for the other person's emotional wellbeing. This empathy further allows us to validate their emotions and show understanding, fostering a sense of trust and mutual respect in the conversation. Being a good conversationalist requires recognizing and understanding others' emotions. By paying attention to nonverbal cues, engaging in active listening, and demonstrating empathy, we can create a supportive and empathetic environment for conversation. This skill not only enhances the quality of our interactions but also helps build meaningful connections and nurtures healthy relationships. By valuing and understanding the emotions of others, we can become more skilled and effective conversationalists.

EMPATHETIC RESPONSE TO EMOTIONAL CUES

Empathy, as a fundamental aspect of human connection, plays a crucial role in our ability to respond effectively to emotional cues during conversations. When engaged in a conversation, it is vital to actively listen, not only to the words uttered by the speaker but also to their emotional undertones. Paying attention to these emotional cues allows us to grasp the unspoken messages and understand the speaker's underlying emotions. By demonstrating empathy through our responses, we can create a safe and nurturing environment that encourages open and honest communication. Empathy involves both understanding the emotions expressed by others and also genuinely feeling and experiencing those emotions alongside them. This deep emotional connection fosters a sense of trust and mutual understanding, leading to a more meaningful and enriching conversation. An empathetic response involves more than just acknowledging the emotions someone is expressing. It requires us to respond in a way that shows we genuinely care and support the person. One way to do this is through validation, which involves acknowledging and affirming the emotions expressed by the speaker. This can be achieved by using phrases such as, "I can understand why you would feel that way" or "It sounds like this situation is really challenging for you". By validating their feelings, we convey that we are actively listening and that their emotions are valid and important. An empathetic response also involves offering comfort and reassurance. When someone opens up about their emotional state, they often seek validation and consolation. By providing words of comfort and reassurance, we can help alleviate their distress and create a sense of understanding and support. Offering phrases like "I'm here for you" or "I believe in your ability to overcome this" can provide the speaker with a renewed sense of hope and encouragement.

Empathy requires the ability to regulate our own emotions and appropriately manage our responses. When faced with intense emotional cues, it is essential to remain composed and level-headed. Reacting impulsively or becoming overwhelmed by emotional stimuli can hinder our ability to provide a supportive and empathetic response. Instead, we should strive to stay present and focused on the speaker's emotions, allowing us to respond thoughtfully and effectively. Empathy is a crucial component of our ability to respond appropriately and empathetically to emotional cues during conversations. By actively listening, acknowledging and validating the emotions expressed, offering comfort and reassurance, and regulating our own emotions, we can create a safe and understanding environment that promotes meaningful and enriching conversations. Empathy goes beyond understanding the words spoken; it involves truly connecting with the speaker on an emotional level, which fosters trust, understanding, and a deeper connection. By cultivating empathy as a conversationalist, we can build stronger relationships and contribute to a more compassionate and empathetic society.

RESPECTING OTHERS' FEELINGS AND OPINIONS

Being a good conversationalist also requires respecting others' feelings and opinions. It is essential to approach conversations with an open mind and the understanding that everyone's perspectives and emotions are valid. This means actively listening to others and valuing their input, even if it differs from our own beliefs. When we respect others' feelings and opinions, we create an atmosphere of inclusivity and mutual respect. This allows for a more meaningful and enriching exchange of ideas. Respecting others' feelings and opinions builds trust and strengthens relationships. People are more likely to engage in open and honest conversations when they feel their thoughts and emotions are acknowledged and respected. On the other hand, disregarding or dismissing another person's feelings and opinions can lead to frustration and conflict. It is important to remember that everyone has had different life experiences that shape their viewpoints, and these differences should be celebrated rather than silenced. Respecting others' feelings and opinions encourages diversity of thought, which is crucial for personal growth and societal progress. By embracing different perspectives, we broaden our own understanding and challenge our assumptions. This fosters a culture of learning and intellectual curiosity. Respecting others' feelings and opinions allows us to become better communicators. When we truly listen to others and validate their thoughts and emotions, we cultivate empathy and emotional intelligence. This enables us to respond more effectively to others' needs and concerns, fostering deeper connections and understanding. It is important to note that respecting others' feelings and opinions does not mean we must agree with everything they say or feel. Disagreements are natural and even healthy in conversations. Our approach should always be rooted in respect and understanding. We can express our differing opinions without belittling or disrespecting others, fostering healthy and productive debates. Becoming a good conversationalist requires a combination of skills and qualities. Actively listening, engaging in meaningful conversations, and respecting others' feelings and opinions are fundamental aspects. These practices not only enhance our communication skills but also contribute to personal growth and stronger relationships. By taking the time to cultivate these skills, we can create dialogues that are enriching, inclusive, and conducive to positive change.

A good conversationalist is someone who possesses the ability to engage in meaningful and stimulating conversations while maintaining a genuine interest in the other person's thoughts and ideas. It is important, as a conversationalist, to be an active listener and to show empathy towards the speaker. Active listening involves focusing on the speaker, maintaining eye contact, and giving verbal and non-verbal cues to show understanding and interest. By doing so, the conversationalist is able to create a safe and welcoming environment, encouraging the speaker to open up and share more of their thoughts and experiences. A good conversationalist should also be knowledgeable on a wide range of topics, enabling them to contribute to the conversation in a meaningful way. This does not mean that one needs to be an expert in every field, but rather, possess a general understanding and curiosity about different subjects. This allows for a diverse and enriching conversation that can be enjoyed by both parties. In addition to knowledge, a good conversationalist should also be able to ask open-ended questions that promote further discussion. These types of questions encourage the speaker to elaborate and provide more detailed responses, allowing the conversation to flow more naturally and deeply. By asking open-ended questions, the conversationalist demonstrates their interest in the speaker's perspective and encourages them to actively participate in the conversation. Alongside asking questions, the good conversationalist should also be mindful of the balance between speaking and listening. While it is important to contribute to the conversation, it is equally important to give the other person ample time to express their thoughts and opinions. Interrupting or dominating the conversation can make the speaker feel disrespected and unimportant. The conversationalist should practice patience and attentiveness, allowing the speaker to feel valued and heard. A good conversationalist must possess emotional intelligence.

Emotional intelligence involves being aware of one's own emotions as well as the emotions of others. This awareness allows the conversationalist to respond appropriately and empathetically to the speaker's experiences, ensuring a positive and supportive conversation. Emotional intelligence enables the conversationalist to navigate sensitive topics with care and sensitivity, avoiding potential misunderstandings or conflicts. Being a good conversationalist is not simply about talking, but rather, about actively engaging with others and creating an environment conducive to deep and meaningful exchanges. By practicing active listening, maintaining a genuine interest in the speaker, being knowledgeable about various topics, asking open-ended questions, finding a healthy balance between speaking and listening, and possessing emotional intelligence, one can become a good conversationalist. Cultivating these skills can not only enhance one's personal relationships but also contribute to a more empathetic and connected society.

VI. BEING RESPECTFUL AND OPEN-MINDED

Another crucial aspect of being a good conversationalist is practicing respect and open-mindedness. Engaging in discussions requires individuals to embrace the diversity of thoughts, beliefs, and opinions. Respectful communication involves acknowledging the viewpoints of others without judgment or condescension, fostering an environment where all ideas are welcomed and valued. Open-mindedness, on the other hand, involves being receptive to new ideas and being willing to adjust one's own perspective based on the information provided. It is imperative to remember that everyone has their own unique experiences and backgrounds that shape their viewpoints. By recognizing this, individuals can approach conversations with an open heart and mind, enabling more productive and meaningful dialogues. Being respectful and open-minded not only shows appreciation for the opinion of others but also encourages the exchange of knowledge and ideas. In order to demonstrate respect during conversations, one must actively listen to the speaker and acknowledge their input. This involves maintaining eye contact, nodding, and providing verbal cues such as "I understand" or "That's a valid point". By actively listening, individuals let the speaker know that their thoughts and ideas are being heard and valued. Refraining from interrupting or dominating conversations also signifies respect for others' opinions. It is important to allow individuals to express their viewpoints fully before offering any response. This allows for a more balanced and equal dialogue, enriching the conversation by incorporating diverse perspectives. Avoiding personal attacks or derogatory remarks is crucial in maintaining a respectful and welcoming atmosphere. By refraining from derogatory language or behaviors, individuals create an environment where everyone feels safe to express their thoughts and opinions freely. In conjunction with respect, open-mindedness is another crucial element of productive discourse. Being open-minded allows individuals to approach conversations with a willingness to consider alternative perspectives. Instead of clinging to preconceived notions or biases, individuals who practice open-mindedness are open to the possibility of learning from others. This can be achieved by seeking to understand different viewpoints and engaging in genuine questioning rather than immediately dismissing them. By doing so, individuals can expand their own perspectives, gain new insights, and foster a deeper appreciation for diversity. Being open-minded enables individuals to adapt their own views based on new information or experiences, ultimately promoting personal growth and development. Being respectful and open-minded are fundamental qualities that a good conversationalist should possess. These qualities create an inclusive and enriching environment where respectful discussions can take place. By actively listening, acknowledging the speaker's input, and refraining from derogatory remarks, individuals can demonstrate respect for others during conversations. Open-mindedness, on the other hand, allows individuals to approach discussions with a willingness to consider different perspectives and learn from others. By practicing respect and open-mindedness, individuals can foster more meaningful connections, gain new insights, and contribute to the creation of a compassionate and open society.

CREATING A SAFE AND INCLUSIVE ENVIRONMENT

In order to be a good conversationalist, it is crucial to establish an atmosphere where all individuals feel comfortable, respected, and valued. This requires actively listening to others without judgment or interruption, acknowledging and validating their perspectives and experiences, and promoting open and honest dialogue. One way to create a safe and inclusive space is by practicing empathy and understanding. This involves placing ourselves in the shoes of others and trying to comprehend their emotions, thoughts, and concerns. By demonstrating empathy, we show genuine interest in others, which encourages them to share their ideas and thoughts more freely. It is important to be aware of our own biases and prejudices that may hinder the inclusivity of our conversations. Recognizing and addressing these biases allows for a more equal and equitable exchange of perspectives. Fostering a sense of psychological safety is vital in creating an atmosphere conducive to productive conversations. This can be achieved by encouraging individuals to express themselves without fear of being misunderstood or belittled. It is crucial to remember that not everyone will feel comfortable speaking up, especially if they feel marginalized or invalidated. As conversationalists, we must actively make an effort to engage those who may be more hesitant to participate in conversations. By doing so, we can create a sense of belonging and inclusivity for all individuals involved. Creating a safe and inclusive environment extends beyond verbal communication. Non-verbal cues such as body language, facial expressions, and tone of voice can play a significant role in how others perceive the safety of a conversation. Being aware of our own non-verbal communication and actively ensuring that it conveys openness and respect is crucial. Being mindful of others' non-verbal cues and responding accordingly can help build trust and understanding. Implementing effective conflict resolution strategies is imperative for maintaining a safe and inclusive environment. Conflict is a natural part of human interaction, and disagreements can arise during conversations. How we handle these conflicts can determine whether the environment remains safe and inclusive. It is crucial to listen attentively, seek to understand different perspectives, and work towards finding common ground. Engaging in healthy debates that are based on mutual respect and the exchange of ideas can lead to personal growth, deeper understanding, and the strengthening of relationships. Creating a safe and inclusive environment is essential for fostering meaningful and productive conversations. Practicing empathy, acknowledging biases, promoting psychological safety, and addressing conflict constructively are all important elements in creating a space where everyone feels heard, respected, and valued. By actively implementing these strategies, we can cultivate an environment that encourages diverse perspectives and allows for personal growth and increased understanding.

VALUING DIFFERENT PERSPECTIVES

In order to engage in meaningful and fruitful conversations, it is crucial to recognize and appreciate the diverse viewpoints and opinions that people bring to the table. By valuing different perspectives, individuals demonstrate their respect for others, their willingness to learn, and their ability to think critically. When engaged in a conversation, it is not enough to simply express one's own ideas and beliefs; it is equally important to listen attentively to the perspectives of others, even if they may differ from our own. Valuing different perspectives allows individuals to broaden their horizons and gain new insights. When one is open to considering alternative viewpoints, they open themselves up to a world of knowledge and diverse experiences. Each person brings their unique background, culture, and life experiences, which inevitably shape their outlook on various topics. By valuing different perspectives, college students can expand their understanding of complex issues, challenge their preconceived notions, and cultivate a well-rounded worldview.

In addition to the intellectual benefits, valuing different perspectives fosters empathy and understanding. Often, individuals may find themselves in conversations with people from different walks of life, with different beliefs and values. Such interactions provide an opportunity to empathize with others and gain a deeper understanding of their experiences and challenges. By embracing diverse perspectives, individuals can promote inclusivity and create a sense of belonging in their conversations, classrooms, and communities. Valuing different perspectives contributes to personal growth and self-awareness. When individuals encounter viewpoints that challenge their own, they are forced to critically analyze their own beliefs, biases, and assumptions. This process of self-reflection helps foster personal growth by enhancing one's capacity for introspection, self-improvement, and personal development. In a college setting, where critical thinking and self-discovery are highly valued, being open-minded and receptive to different perspectives can greatly enhance one's intellectual and personal growth.

Valuing different perspectives has the potential to cultivate collaborative problem-solving. In today's complex and interconnected world, finding solutions to global challenges requires collaboration and the ability to harness the collective wisdom of diverse individuals. By embracing different perspectives, college students can enhance their ability to work collaboratively with others, build bridges, and find innovative solutions to complex problems. Valuing different perspectives is a crucial skill for being a good conversationalist. By recognizing and appreciating the diverse viewpoints and opinions of others, individuals not only enhance their intellectual growth but also foster empathy, understanding, and personal development. Valuing different perspectives has the potential to promote collaboration and innovation, which are essential skills in the modern world. In order to truly engage in meaningful and enriching conversations, it is imperative to cultivate an attitude of openness and respect towards different perspectives.

PRACTICING CULTURAL SENSITIVITY

Another important aspect of being a good conversationalist is practicing cultural sensitivity. In our increasingly diverse and interconnected world, it is crucial to understand and appreciate different cultural customs, values, and norms. Cultural sensitivity refers to the ability to communicate and interact effectively with individuals from diverse backgrounds, while being respectful and considerate of their beliefs and perspectives. This involves recognizing and valuing cultural differences, avoiding stereotypes and prejudices, and adapting one's communication style to accommodate different cultural norms. Practicing cultural sensitivity not only promotes understanding and harmony among individuals from different cultural backgrounds, but it also fosters a more inclusive and welcoming environment for everyone involved in the conversation. To begin with, practicing cultural sensitivity requires an open and unbiased mindset. One should approach conversations with the intention of learning and gaining insights into different cultures, rather than imposing their own beliefs and values onto others. This entails actively listening to others and being receptive to their perspectives, even if they differ from one's own. By adopting this attitude, individuals can foster a respectful and inclusive conversation where all participants feel valued and heard. Being aware of cultural differences and avoiding stereotypes is essential for practicing cultural sensitivity. Stereotypes are generalizations or assumptions made about a particular group based on their cultural background. Engaging in conversations without relying on stereotypes requires individuals to approach each person as an individual, rather than making assumptions based on their cultural identity. This not only enables individuals to have a deeper and more meaningful understanding of others, but it also helps to break down barriers and promote a sense of inclusivity and acceptance.

Another aspect of cultural sensitivity is adapting one's communication style to accommodate different cultural norms. Communication styles vary across cultures, with some cultures valuing direct and assertive communication, while others emphasize indirect and polite communication. Being sensitive to these differences and adjusting one's approach accordingly can significantly enhance the effectiveness of a conversation. Individuals should be mindful of non-verbal cues, such as body language and gestures, which can also differ across cultures. By being attentive to these nuances, individuals can ensure that their communication is respectful, clear, and easily understood by all participants. Practicing cultural sensitivity is vital for being a good conversationalist. By embracing an open mindset, avoiding stereotypes, and adapting one's communication style to accommodate different cultural norms, individuals can foster inclusive and respectful conversations. Developing cultural sensitivity not only promotes understanding and appreciation of diverse cultures, but it also helps to create a more harmonious and interconnected world. As our society becomes increasingly multicultural, practicing cultural sensitivity is not only a valuable skill but a responsibility we should all uphold.

AVOIDING INTERRUPTING OR DOMINATING THE CONVERSATION

Another crucial aspect of being a good conversationalist is avoiding interrupting or dominating the conversation. Interrupting someone while they are expressing their thoughts or ideas is not only rude but also signifies a lack of respect for the other person's opinions. It is essential to listen attentively and patiently, allowing the speaker to finish their train of thought before interjecting with our own thoughts or statements. By doing so, we show that we value and appreciate their perspective, fostering a positive and respectful atmosphere for open dialogue. Dominating the conversation by constantly steering it towards our own interests or experiences can hinder meaningful communication. Conversations should be a two-way street where both parties have equal opportunities to contribute and share their thoughts. Dominating the conversation not only suppresses the opinions and insights of others but also hampers the development of genuine connections and understanding. Instead, we should aim to create a balanced exchange by allowing all participants to take turns in expressing their thoughts and contributing to the dialogue. Practicing active listening skills, such as nodding, maintaining eye contact, and providing affirmations, can help prevent interruptions and foster a more inclusive conversational environment. To avoid interrupting or dominating the conversation, it is essential to be mindful of our communication style and recognize when our actions may be hindering the flow of conversation. One effective strategy is to wait for a natural pause in the conversation before interjecting. This allows the speaker to complete their point and demonstrates our willingness to listen attentively. We should strive to be aware of our non-verbal cues, as they can convey a message of interest or impatience. For instance, crossing our arms or constantly checking our watch sends signals of disinterest, potentially discouraging the speaker from sharing their thoughts freely. To combat this, maintaining an open posture and showing genuine interest through active engagement can encourage others to participate actively in the conversation, resulting in a more enriching exchange of ideas. It is important to acknowledge that conversations should not solely revolve around our own interests and experiences. Embracing a diverse range of perspectives can broaden our own understanding and spark stimulating discussions. By actively encouraging others to share their thoughts and asking open-ended questions, we create opportunities for different viewpoints to be expressed. Supporting and appreciating the contributions of others further establishes a collaborative and respectful conversational environment. By avoiding interrupting or dominating the conversation, we foster inclusivity, respect, and meaningful dialogue that allows for personal growth and the cultivation of genuine connections.

ALLOWING OTHERS TO EXPRESS THEIR THOUGHTS

In order to be a good conversationalist, it is essential to cultivate the skill of allowing others to express their thoughts. This involves creating an environment where individuals feel comfortable sharing their opinions, ideas, and perspectives. One key aspect of this skill is active listening, which requires giving one's full attention to the speaker and demonstrating genuine interest in their thoughts. Active listening involves not only hearing what the other person is saying but also comprehending it and responding appropriately. It is crucial to avoid interrupting or rushing others when they are speaking, as this can hinder their ability to fully convey their ideas. Instead, one should practice patience and be willing to let others express themselves fully before interjecting with their own thoughts. It is important to be non-judgmental and remain open-minded when others share their opinions, even if they differ from one's own. This entails suspending personal biases and preconceived notions in order to understand and appreciate diverse perspectives. By doing so, one fosters an inclusive atmosphere that encourages the free flow of ideas and promotes constructive dialogue. Allowing others to express their thoughts necessitates creating a safe space where individuals feel respected and valued. This involves refraining from demeaning or dismissing others' opinions, even if they may seem unconventional or contradictory. Instead, one should strive to foster an environment that celebrates diverse perspectives and encourages a healthy exchange of ideas. It is crucial to avoid dominating conversations and monopolizing the speaking time. Instead, one should actively encourage others to contribute to the conversation and provide opportunities for them to express their thoughts. This can be achieved by asking open-ended questions, inviting others to share their experiences, or seeking clarification on their viewpoints. By doing so, individuals feel empowered and acknowledged, leading to a more balanced and engaging conversation. Allowing others to express their thoughts requires empathetic communication. This involves not only understanding and acknowledging their ideas but also appreciating the emotions and experiences that underlie their perspectives. By demonstrating empathy, one shows genuine care and understanding towards others, which in turn strengthens interpersonal connections and fosters meaningful conversations. Allowing others to express their thoughts is a fundamental aspect of being a good conversationalist. By practicing active listening, remaining non-judgmental, creating a safe space, encouraging participation, and demonstrating empathy, individuals can cultivate an inclusive and engaging environment that promotes constructive dialogue and meaningful connections. These skills not only contribute to effective communication but also enrich personal relationships and broaden one's knowledge and understanding of the world.

ENCOURAGING BALANCED PARTICIPATION

Encouraging balanced participation is paramount in becoming a good conversationalist. A conversation is a two-way street, and both parties should have the opportunity to contribute and share their thoughts and ideas. It is not uncommon for certain individuals to dominate the conversation, leaving little room for others to express themselves. To prevent this from happening, one must be mindful of their own speaking time and actively encourage others to participate. One effective technique is to ask open-ended questions that invite diverse perspectives. These questions can foster a more inclusive environment and allow different individuals to provide their input. By demonstrating a genuine interest in what others have to say, a good conversationalist can create a space where all participants feel valued and heard. Actively listening to others can also encourage balanced participation. Instead of being solely focused on formulating your own response, it is crucial to give undivided attention to the speaker. This not only shows respect but also allows one to better understand the viewpoint being shared. Paraphrasing or summarizing what the speaker said can promote deeper engagement and encourage them to expand on their thoughts. This active listening technique fosters a collaborative conversation where all participants have the chance to contribute equally. Another aspect to consider when encouraging balanced participation is being aware of non-verbal cues. Paying attention to body language can help recognize when someone wants to speak but may be hesitant. For example, if an individual seems eager to interject but is constantly interrupted or glanced over, they may become discouraged from participating further. To address this, a good conversationalist can practice inclusivity by consciously creating opportunities for others to speak. This can be as simple as pausing after making a point, giving others a chance to respond or sharing the spotlight by acknowledging and highlighting their contributions. A good conversationalist can actively moderate and manage the conversation to ensure balanced participation. This includes redirecting the conversation if it becomes one-sided or inviting quieter participants to share their thoughts. By playing a proactive role in guiding the discourse and ensuring everyone's voice is heard, a good conversationalist can foster an environment that encourages balanced participation. A good conversationalist understands the importance of encouraging balanced participation. By asking open-ended questions, actively listening, being aware of non-verbal cues, and actively managing the conversation, a good conversationalist promotes an inclusive environment where all participants have the opportunity to express themselves and contribute. By practicing these techniques, one can become a better conversationalist and create meaningful interactions that foster mutual understanding and respect. To be a good conversationalist, one must possess several key qualities. First and foremost, active listening is essential. This means being fully present in the conversation, attentively engaging with the speaker, and responding thoughtfully. By actively listening, one demonstrates respect and validation for the other person's views and ideas, fostering a sense of connection and understanding. A good conversationalist is knowledgeable and well-informed on a wide range of topics. This allows them to contribute valuable insights and engage in meaningful discussions. It is important to stay informed through reading, research, and staying up-to-date with current events. By being knowledgeable, one can add depth and substance to conversations, making them more enriching and enlightening for both parties involved. A good conversationalist is open-minded and receptive to new ideas and perspectives. They understand the value of diverse viewpoints and are willing to step outside of their comfort zone to explore new concepts and challenge their own beliefs. This fosters intellectual growth and allows for stimulating conversations that can lead to personal develop-ment. A good conversationalist is empathetic and understand-ing. They strive to see things from the other person's point of view and are sensitive to their emotions and experiences. By showing empathy, one creates a safe and supportive environ-ment for open and honest communication. This can lead to deeper connections and meaningful relationships. In addition, a good conversationalist is skilled in asking insightful questions. This helps to keep the conversation flowing and allows for a deeper exploration of topics. Asking open-ended questions en-courages the other person to share more about themselves or their thoughts, fostering a sense of trust and rapport. A good conversationalist is mindful of non-verbal cues and body lan-guage. They understand that communication is not solely reliant on words, but also on gestures, facial expressions, and tone of voice. By being attentive to non-verbal cues, one can better un-derstand the underlying emotions and intentions of the speaker. This enables a more nuanced and effective response, enhancing the overall quality of the conversation. Being a good conversa-tionalist requires active listening, knowledge, open-mindedness, empathy, insightful questioning, and attentiveness to non-verbal cues. Developing these qualities takes time and practice, but the

rewards are well worth the effort. By becoming a skilled conversationalist, one can cultivate deeper connections, foster intellectual growth, and create a more inclusive and understanding society.

VII. USING EFFECTIVE COMMUNICATION TECHNIQUES

Effective communication skills are essential in becoming a good conversationalist. These skills involve more than just being able to speak clearly and articulately; they encompass a wide range of techniques that can enhance any conversation. One of the most crucial techniques is active listening. Active listening is the ability to fully concentrate on and understand what the other person is saying, rather than just waiting for your turn to speak. It requires being present in the moment and giving your full attention to the speaker. By demonstrating active listening, you convey genuine interest and respect for the other person's thoughts and opinions, which can foster a deeper connection and more meaningful conversation. Another important technique in effective communication is asking open-ended questions. Open-ended questions encourage the speaker to elaborate and provide more detailed responses, thereby expanding the conversation. These types of questions avoid simple "yes" or "no" answers and instead promote a deeper exploration of topics. Open-ended questions demonstrate your curiosity and desire to understand the other person's perspective, leading to a more engaging and inclusive discussion. Conversely, closed-ended questions should be avoided, as they tend to limit the conversation and rarely stimulate meaningful dialogue.

Body language plays a significant role in effective communication. Nonverbal cues, such as facial expressions, hand gestures, and body posture, can convey a wealth of information and influence the tone of a conversation. Maintaining eye contact, for instance, shows attentiveness and interest, while crossing arms or avoiding eye contact may indicate disinterest or disagreement. By being aware of your own body language and observing that of others, you can more effectively gauge the feelings and intentions behind the words being spoken, allowing for a more empathetic and impactful conversation. Using appropriate language is crucial for effective communication. This involves tailoring your vocabulary and tone to match the situation and the person you are conversing with. Avoiding jargon or technical terms that may not be understood by the listener is important, as it ensures clarity and comprehension. Using a friendly and respectful tone can help create a positive atmosphere, encouraging openness and receptiveness. Being mindful of your language and adapting it to the specific context can significantly improve the quality of your conversations.

Being mindful of cultural differences is essential when engaging in effective communication. Cultural norms and expectations can vary greatly from person to person, and being sensitive to these differences can help avoid misunderstandings and promote inclusion and understanding. This includes being aware of nonverbal cues, such as personal space preferences, as well as being respectful of different communication styles and customs. By embracing diversity and adapting to various cultural contexts, you can facilitate more successful and harmonious conversations. Effective communication techniques are integral to being a good conversationalist. Active listening, asking open-ended questions, utilizing appropriate body language and language, and being mindful of cultural differences all contribute to engaging and meaningful conversations. By honing these skills, individuals can enhance their communication abilities and build stronger connections with others, fostering understanding and empathy in every interaction.

CLARITY AND CONCISENESS

Clarity and conciseness are fundamental elements of effective communication. When engaging in a conversation, it is crucial to express oneself in a clear and concise manner to ensure that our message is accurately understood by the listeners. Clarity refers to the ability to articulate our thoughts and ideas in a way that is easily comprehensible. This entails selecting the right words, organizing our thoughts coherently, and avoiding ambiguous statements or jargon. By choosing our words carefully, we can convey our message more effectively and eliminate any confusion that may arise. Organizing our thoughts in a clear and logical manner allows our listeners to follow our train of thought, promoting a more productive and engaging conversation. Conversely, a lack of clarity in communication can lead to misinterpretation, misinformation, and Breakdowns in understanding between the speaker and the listener. Conciseness, on the other hand, refers to expressing our message in a succinct and efficient manner. It involves eliminating unnecessary details, tangents, and repetitious statements that can hinder the clarity and flow of our communication. By being concise, we respect the time and attention of our conversation partners, ensuring that our message gets across without overwhelming or boring them. This skill can be particularly beneficial in group discussions or presentations, where time is limited, and multiple perspectives need to be heard. Concise communication demonstrates our ability to prioritize information, recognizing the most crucial points of discussion and presenting them in a concise manner.

By doing so, we help our listeners focus on the core aspects of our message, increasing their engagement and understanding. Clarity and conciseness go hand in hand when striving to be a good conversationalist. A clear message but lacking conciseness can result in a loss of interest or attention from our listeners. Conversely, a concise yet unclear message can lead to confusion and a lack of understanding. Thus, it is essential to strike a balance between the two, tailoring our communication to suit the needs of the conversation, the listeners, and the context.

To achieve clarity and conciseness in our conversations, it is necessary to practice active listening. By attentively listening to our conversation partners, we can identify any points of confusion or areas that require further explanation. Paraphrasing and summarizing the main points of discussion can help ensure that we have correctly understood and interpreted the information provided. It is crucial to seek feedback and clarification when necessary, as this enables us to address any potential misunderstandings or misconceptions promptly.

Clarity and conciseness are essential facets of effective communication. By expressing ourselves in a clear and concise manner, we enhance understanding, engagement, and overall communication. Active listening and seeking feedback can help us fine-tune our communication skills, ensuring that our conversations are meaningful, productive, and enjoyable for all parties involved.

ORGANIZING THOUGHTS BEFORE SPEAKING

Organizing thoughts before speaking is a crucial aspect of being a good conversationalist. It entails taking the time to structure one's ideas in a clear and concise manner before articulating them verbally. This practice allows for effective communication, as it minimizes the chances of misinterpretation or confusion during conversations. By organizing their thoughts before speaking, individuals can foster meaningful and engaging discussions, as they can convey their ideas with clarity and coherence. Organizing thoughts before speaking also demonstrates respect for the other person's time and attention, as it ensures that the speaker is prepared and ready to deliver their message effectively. One key benefit of organizing thoughts before speaking is the ability to provide thoughtful and well-reasoned responses during conversations. This practice allows individuals to gather their ideas and filter out any irrelevant or unnecessary information before sharing their opinions or insights. By doing so, they can ensure that their contributions are both relevant and valuable, enhancing the overall quality of the conversation. Organizing thoughts beforehand helps individuals to better articulate their viewpoints, supporting them with appropriate evidence or examples. This not only aids in effective communication but also establishes credibility, as their ideas are presented in a logical and coherent manner. Another advantage of organizing thoughts before speaking is the prevention of confusion or miscommunication. When thoughts are not organized, individuals may struggle to express themselves clearly, leading to misunderstandings or the need for repeated explanations. This can frustrate both the speaker and the listener, potentially derailing the conversation and hindering the flow of ideas. By taking the time to structure their thoughts, individuals can eliminate unnecessary digressions or tangents, thus ensuring that their message is concise and easily understood by others.

Organizing thoughts before speaking demonstrates respect for the listener's time and attention. In a conversation, individuals should strive to express their ideas efficiently and succinctly to maintain the other person's engagement. When thoughts are disorganized, it can lead to rambling or incoherent speech, which may cause the listener to lose interest or become distracted. By organizing thoughts before speaking, individuals can deliver their message in a focused and concise manner, respecting the listener's time and enabling efficient communication.

Organizing thoughts before speaking is a fundamental component of being a good conversationalist. This practice allows individuals to provide thoughtful and well-reasoned responses while minimizing the chances of miscommunication. Organizing thoughts demonstrates respect for the listener's time and engagement, ensuring that the conversation remains engaging and meaningful. By engaging in this practice, individuals can enhance their communication skills, fostering meaningful and productive conversations with others.

SUMMARIZING AND PARAPHRASING WHEN NECESSARY

Summarizing and paraphrasing are essential skills for effective communication, particularly in conversations where the exchange of ideas and information is valued. Summarizing involves condensing the main points or ideas of a text or conversation into a concise and coherent form, while paraphrasing focuses on rephrasing the information in a way that retains its meaning but using different words or sentence structures. These techniques are particularly useful when engaging in discussions or debates, as they allow individuals to demonstrate comprehension and engage with the topic at hand. When summarizing, one must first identify the key points or arguments being made. This requires careful listening and attention to detail, as well as the ability to discern the most salient information. By synthesizing these main ideas, the speaker can then provide a concise overview of the discussion, enabling others to engage with the content without having to sift through excessive details or tangents. Summarizing also allows for more efficient communication, as it enables individuals to convey complex information within a limited time frame. Summarizing demonstrates active listening and engagement, as it shows that one has not only understood the conversation but has also taken the time to distill its essence.

On the other hand, paraphrasing involves rephrasing someone else's words or ideas while retaining the original meaning. This technique is particularly useful when one wishes to clarify a point or respond to a statement made by another person. By rephrasing the content, individuals can not only demonstrate their understanding but also contribute to the conversation by providing a fresh perspective or insight. Paraphrasing also allows for more effective communication, as it enables individuals to convey the same message using their own words, catering to different learning styles and enhancing overall comprehension.

While summarizing and paraphrasing are valuable tools for communication, it is important to use them appropriately and ethically. Plagiarism is a serious offense in any academic or professional setting, and it is crucial to give credit to the original source when summarizing or paraphrasing the ideas of others. One should also be mindful of accuracy and intent, striving to convey the original ideas as faithfully as possible while avoiding misinterpretation or misrepresentation.

Summarizing and paraphrasing are critical skills for effective communication and conversation. They allow individuals to demonstrate comprehension, engage with the topic at hand, and contribute to the exchange of ideas and information. By summarizing, one can condense complex information into a concise form, while paraphrasing enables individuals to rephrase information in their own words. It is crucial to use these techniques appropriately and ethically, acknowledging the original source and striving for accuracy. These skills enable individuals to be more effective conversationalists, fostering thoughtful and meaningful exchanges that lead to mutual understanding and growth.

TAILORING COMMUNICATION STYLE TO THE AUDIENCE

Each individual possesses unique characteristics, beliefs, and cultural backgrounds that shape their communication preferences and expectations. To effectively connect with others, it is important to adapt one's communication style accordingly. Firstly, understanding the audience is vital in tailoring communication. Age, educational background, and profession are factors that significantly influence the way people communicate. For instance, when conversing with a group of college students, utilizing informal language and incorporating pop culture references may enhance engagement and relatability. On the other hand, when communicating with professionals in a formal context, using industry-specific terminology and maintaining a polished demeanor would be more appropriate. Secondly, recognizing cultural differences is essential in adjusting communication style. When conversing with individuals from diverse cultural backgrounds, it is vital to respect and understand their customs, norms, and verbal cues. For instance, in many Eastern cultures, individuals may rely heavily on nonverbal cues such as facial expressions and body language to understand the speaker's intent. In contrast, Western cultures may prioritize direct and explicit communication. Adapting one's communication approach to accommodate such differences fosters inclusivity and facilitates effective conversations. Recognizing the individual needs of the audience allows for effective tailoring of communication style. Psychographic factors, such as personality traits and interests, significantly impact communication preferences. For instance, introverted individuals may prefer more reflective and one-on-one conversations, whereas extroverted individuals may thrive in group discussions and social events. By considering these factors, conversationalists can cater to the unique needs and preferences of their audience, thereby establishing rapport and facilitating meaningful conversations. Adapting communication style is more than just conforming to others' preferences; it is also about building empathy and fostering understanding. When conversationalists make a conscious effort to understand their audience, they create an environment of inclusivity and genuine connection. Tailoring communication allows individuals to overcome communication barriers and bridge gaps amongst diverse groups of people. The ability to adapt communication style to the audience is a powerful skill that can enhance relationships, professional opportunities, and personal growth. Tailoring communication style to the audience is an indispensable aspect of mastering the art of conversation. By recognizing the audience's characteristics, understanding cultural differences, and adjusting communication approaches to meet individual needs, conversationalists can create meaningful connections and facilitate productive conversations. Adapting communication style fosters empathy, inclusion, and understanding amongst diverse groups of people. Individuals aspiring to be good conversationalists should prioritize tailoring their communication style to the audience, as it contributes significantly to successful interactions and fosters personal growth.

ADAPTING TO DIFFERENT PERSONALITIES AND BACKGROUNDS

One important aspect of being a good conversationalist is the ability to adapt to different personalities and backgrounds. In any given conversation, it is highly likely that individuals from diverse backgrounds with varying personalities will be present. It is crucial to possess the skill of adaptability in order to effectively communicate and connect with others. Adapting to different personalities requires the art of understanding and empathy. It involves being able to recognize and appreciate the unique traits of individuals, and adjusting one's approach accordingly. For example, if someone is introverted and reserved, it may be necessary to take a more gentle and patient approach, allowing them time to open up and share their thoughts. On the other hand, if someone is more extroverted and outgoing, it may be important to match their energy and enthusiasm in order to establish a rapport. Adapting to different backgrounds encompasses a broader understanding of cultural and social diversity. It requires a willingness to learn and appreciate the values, beliefs, and customs of others. This involves being open-minded and respectful, avoiding assumptions or stereotypes that may hinder genuine connections. An effective way to adapt to different backgrounds is through active listening. By actively listening to others, we can gain a deeper understanding of their experiences and perspectives. This enables us to engage in meaningful and respectful conversations that foster empathy and mutual understanding. Being adaptable to different personalities and backgrounds is closely linked to effective communication skills.

The ability to communicate effectively involves not only speaking, but also understanding non-verbal cues and body language. This includes being attentive to facial expressions, gestures, and tone of voice. By paying attention to these nuances, we can adjust our communication style to ensure that we are effectively conveying our thoughts and connecting with others. Another important aspect of adapting to different personalities and backgrounds is being aware of our own biases and prejudices. It is essential to approach conversations with an open mind and without preconceived notions. This requires self-reflection and a commitment to continuously challenge our own assumptions and beliefs. By doing so, we are able to engage in more meaningful and respectful conversations that foster understanding and connection. Being a good conversationalist necessitates the ability to adapt to different personalities and backgrounds. This entails understanding and appreciating the uniqueness of individuals, actively listening, and effectively communicating. It involves being open-minded and respectful, and constantly challenging our own biases and assumptions. By cultivating these skills, we can create conversations that are inclusive, meaningful, and ultimately foster connections among diverse individuals.

USING APPROPRIATE LANGUAGE AND TONE

Another important aspect of being a good conversationalist is using appropriate language and tone. The choice of language and tone can greatly influence the effectiveness of our communication and the way others perceive us. It is essential to adapt our language depending on the context and the person we are talking to. Using overly complex or technical language might result in confusion or alienation of the listener, while using slang or informal language might be inappropriate in a professional setting. The tone of our conversation should also be considered. A harsh or condescending tone can easily offend others and hinder the flow of a conversation. On the other hand, an overly timid or passive tone might prevent us from expressing our thoughts and opinions effectively. Striking a balance between being assertive and respectful is key. A good conversationalist should aim to speak with clarity, confidence, and consideration. By using language and tone appropriately, we can establish a positive atmosphere for communication and effectively convey our ideas to others. A good conversationalist possesses a crucial skill that allows them to effortlessly connect with others, fostering an atmosphere of engagement and understanding. This skill is active listening—a technique that involves fully focusing on the speaker, grasping their words, and responding accordingly. To become a master conversationalist, one must develop the ability to actively listen, particularly by employing techniques such as maintaining eye contact, providing nonverbal cues, and practicing empathy. First and foremost, maintaining eye contact is essential in demonstrating genuine attentiveness during a conversation. By maintaining eye contact, one exhibits their commitment to the discussion, making the speaker feel respected and valued. Eye contact helps to establish a connection on a deeper level, solidifying the bond between the conversationalists and encouraging transparent communication. Providing nonverbal cues, such as nods and smiles, can indicate understanding and encouragement, creating a positive and inclusive conversation space. These cues offer the speaker reassurance, conveying that their thoughts and feelings are being acknowledged and appreciated. Consequently, a conversationalist who actively uses nonverbal cues establishes a rapport that fosters open and free-flowing communication. Practicing empathy is imperative when aiming to become an active listener. Empathy enables an individual to understand and share the feelings of another, creating a space where the speaker can express themselves authentically, knowing that they are being heard and understood. Demonstrating empathy can be as simple as using phrases such as "I understand how you feel" or "That must have been difficult for you". These expressions of empathy not only validate the speaker's emotions but also encourage further exploration and elaboration, leading to deeper and more meaningful conversations. Active listening is an essential skill for anyone striving to become a good conversationalist. By actively listening, individuals can demonstrate their respect and value for the speaker, foster a strong connection through eye contact, provide nonverbal cues to encourage open communication, and practice empathy to create a profound understanding of the speaker's thoughts and emotions. It is important to remember that acquiring these skills requires practice and self-awareness. It is recommended that individuals dedicate time and effort to develop their active listening abilities in order to enhance their conversational skills and build more fruitful connections with others. In doing so, they will discover that mastering the art of active listening not only enriches their own lives by allowing them to develop deeper relationships but also creates a positive impact on the lives of those around them.

VIII. BUILDING RAPPORT AND CONNECTION

Building rapport and connection is an essential aspect of being a good conversationalist. Rapport refers to the harmonious connection and understanding between two individuals, while connection entails the establishment of a deeper bond based on shared values, experiences, and emotions. To effectively build rapport, it is crucial to cultivate active listening skills and show genuine interest in the other person. Active listening involves giving undivided attention, maintaining eye contact, and providing verbal and nonverbal cues that indicate attentiveness and understanding. Asking open-ended questions and seeking clarifications demonstrate a sincere desire to engage in meaningful dialogue, fostering a stronger connection. By demonstrating empathy, one can validate the other person's emotions and experiences, thereby creating a safe and supportive environment for open communication. Another important aspect of building rapport and connection lies in finding common ground or shared interests. Identifying shared experiences or hobbies provides a solid foundation upon which to establish a connection and strengthen the bond between conversational partners. Individuals can tap into their own experiences, ideas, and emotions to establish a relatable and genuine connection. Sharing personal stories or anecdotes with vulnerability not only creates a sense of trust but also allows for a deeper understanding of each other. By being authentic and open, one can inspire reciprocation from the other person, resulting in a more meaningful and enjoyable conversation. Nonverbal communication also plays a significant role in building rapport and connection. Nonverbal cues such as facial expressions, body language, and tone of voice can convey emotions, intentions, and interest. Maintaining appropriate eye contact, smiling, and using a warm and friendly tone contribute to the establishment of a positive ambiance and encourage a favorable response from the other person. Acknowledging and reflecting the other person's body language can also create a sense of comfort, as it implies mirroring and understanding.

Building rapport and connection requires one's ability to adapt to various communication styles and preferences. Each individual has distinct ways of expressing themselves, so it is important to be adaptable and flexible in one's conversational approach. By adjusting one's communication style to accommodate the other person's preferences, one can create a more comfortable and engaging environment for both parties involved. Taking note of cultural and social differences can further enhance the rapport and connection between individuals, as it demonstrates respect and understanding of diverse perspectives and backgrounds.

Building rapport and connection is a crucial aspect of being a good conversationalist. Through active listening, genuine interest, empathy, finding common ground, sharing personal stories, utilizing nonverbal cues, and adapting to different communication styles, individuals can foster a stronger and more meaningful connection with others. Building rapport and connection not only enriches conversations but also paves the way for long-lasting relationships and a deeper understanding of one another. By honing these skills, individuals can elevate their conversational abilities and enhance their overall interpersonal effectiveness.

FINDING COMMON INTERESTS OR TOPICS

To be a good conversationalist, it is important to find common interests or topics that both parties can engage in. Engaging in conversations about shared interests creates a strong foundation for meaningful and enjoyable conversations. Common interests or topics serve as a starting point for building a connection between individuals and can help to establish a sense of rapport. When people discover shared hobbies, experiences, or passions, they often feel more comfortable and open in their conversations. Finding these commonalities allows each person to contribute to the conversation, and as a result, the dialogue becomes more dynamic and engaging. Discussing shared interests can strengthen the bond between conversational partners as they realize that they are not alone in their preferences or experiences. Finding common interests or topics can serve as an icebreaker, helping to alleviate any initial awkwardness or tension. By identifying mutual interests, individuals can find a common ground upon which they can initiate and carry the conversation forward. This shared platform allows them to appreciate each other's perspectives and insights, fostering a more inclusive and interactive discussion. Whether it is a favorite book, a similar travel experience, or a shared hobby, discussing these commonalities paves the way for a smoother conversation.

Exploring common interests or topics opens the door to new and different perspectives. In conversing about shared passions, people often learn new information or gain fresh insights that they may not have previously considered. By being receptive to the views and experiences of others, individuals can broaden their knowledge and understanding of a particular subject. This exchange of ideas creates a dynamic interplay in the conversation and ultimately enhances the overall quality of the interaction. Finding common interests can be a way to bridge gaps and foster understanding between individuals from diverse backgrounds or with differing opinions. In an increasingly interconnected world, it is essential to be able to engage in conversations with people who may have different perspectives or beliefs. By searching for shared interests or topics, individuals can find common ground upon which they can build mutual respect and establish a basis for further discussion. In a time when the world seems increasingly divided, finding these commonalities can serve as a powerful tool to promote empathy, understanding, and unity. Finding common interests or topics is essential to being a good conversationalist. It provides a foundation for a meaningful and enjoyable conversation, serves as an icebreaker, facilitates the exchange of different perspectives, and bridges gaps between individuals. By actively seeking out shared passions or experiences, individuals can create an environment that encourages engagement, openness, and connection. Through these conversations, people can form lasting bonds, broaden their horizons, and contribute to a more inclusive and understanding society. Thus, finding common interests is a vital skill to possess when engaging in conversations with others.

ENGAGING WITH SHARED EXPERIENCES

Engaging with shared experiences is an essential component of being a good conversationalist. When individuals connect over commonalities, it creates a sense of camaraderie and allows for the establishment of a deeper rapport. By sharing experiences, whether they be joys, sorrows, or even mundane occurrences, conversations become more meaningful and authentic. Shared experiences serve as a foundation for empathetic connections, as they provide a common ground from which individuals can relate to one another. When engaging with shared experiences, it is important to actively listen and show genuine interest in the other person's stories. Through active listening, one can validate the speaker's emotions and demonstrate empathy, further strengthening the bonds of the conversation.

Engaging with shared experiences also allows for the development of a sense of belonging. Feeling understood and accepted is a fundamental human need, and sharing experiences with others fulfills this need. When individuals find common ground in their experiences, they feel a sense of kinship and validation, fostering a deeper connection. This sense of belonging has numerous positive effects on individual well-being and mental health. It cultivates a sense of purpose and community, reducing feelings of isolation and loneliness. Engaging with shared experiences can help individuals gain new perspectives and broaden their horizons. Through exposure to diverse experiences and viewpoints, one can develop a greater understanding and appreciation for the world around them.

Engaging with shared experiences allows for the exchange of

knowledge and wisdom. Conversations centered around shared experiences provide opportunities for learning and growth. By actively participating in these discussions, individuals can gain insights and advice from others who have been through similar situations. Shared experiences act as a source of collective wisdom, enabling individuals to navigate their own challenges with greater confidence and resilience. This aspect of engaging with shared experiences makes conversations not only enjoyable but also intellectually stimulating. It is important to note that engaging with shared experiences does not imply solely focusing on similarities. Embracing differences and diverse perspectives is equally important in fostering engaging conversations. While shared experiences can be a powerful starting point, conversations can be enriched by exploring unique aspects of each individual's experiences. This helps to challenge assumptions, broaden understanding, and encourage personal growth.

Engaging with shared experiences is crucial in becoming a good conversationalist. It fosters connection, belonging, and empathy. By actively listening and showing genuine interest, individuals can create a safe space for open and authentic conversations. Shared experiences provide a foundation for mutual understanding, knowledge exchange, and personal growth. It is equally important to embrace differences and diverse perspectives, allowing conversations to transcend the limitations of common experiences. In doing so, individuals can develop deeper connections, broaden their horizons, and become more well-rounded conversationalists.

IDENTIFYING COMMON GOALS OR VALUES

Identifying common goals or values is a key component of being a good conversationalist. When engaging in conversation, it is important to seek out common ground to establish a sense of connection and understanding between individuals. Common goals or values act as a bridge, allowing for a more meaningful and impactful exchange of ideas, opinions, and experiences. By identifying shared objectives or belief systems, conversationalists can navigate conversations with greater ease, as they have a foundation on which to build upon. This not only fosters a more inclusive and collaborative dialogue but also encourages the exploration of different perspectives and the exchange of knowledge. One of the main benefits of identifying common goals or values within a conversation is the creation of a strong sense of camaraderie and mutual respect. By finding areas of agreement, conversationalists establish a foundation of trust, which in turn facilitates open and honest communication. This, in essence, allows for the formation of a positive rapport, where individuals feel comfortable expressing their thoughts and ideas without fear of judgment or criticism. When conversationalists share common goals or values, they are more likely to listen attentively and engage in active and empathetic listening. This not only fosters meaningful connections but also encourages the development of deeper relationships based on trust and understanding. Identifying common goals or values helps to bridge societal and cultural divides, promoting inclusivity and a sense of belonging within a conversation. In our increasingly diverse world, conversations involving individuals from different back-grounds and perspectives can present challenges in finding common ground. By focusing on shared objectives or values, conversationalists can transcend these differences and foster a more harmonious and respectful exchange. By recognizing shared goals, individuals can find commonalities that may not have been immediately apparent and engage in a meaningful discussion centered around these shared interests. This not only creates a more inclusive conversation but also promotes a sense of acceptance and understanding between individuals from diverse backgrounds. Identifying common goals or values within a conversation encourages the exploration and exchange of different perspectives. While similarities can create connections, it is also important to recognize and embrace differences in opinions and beliefs. By acknowledging shared objectives, conversationalists can approach disagreements more constructively, focusing on finding solutions or compromises rather than engaging in heated debates. This helps to foster a culture of open-mindedness and intellectual growth within conversations, where different viewpoints are encouraged and valued. By actively seeking out common goals or values, conversationalists open themselves up to new perspectives and insights that they might not have considered otherwise. Identifying common goals or values is vital in becoming a good conversationalist. It allows for the establishment of a strong sense of camaraderie and mutual respect, bridging cultural and societal divides and promoting inclusivity within conversations. It encourages the exploration and exchange of different perspectives, fostering intellectual growth and a deeper understanding of others. By identifying common goals or values, conversationalists create a solid foundation upon which meaningful and impactful conversations can be built.

SHOWING GENUINE CURIOSITY ABOUT OTHERS

In today's fast-paced world, people often find themselves pre-occupied with their own thoughts and concerns, which can hinder their ability to engage in meaningful conversations. By developing a genuine curiosity about others, individuals can not only foster stronger connections with people but also gain valuable insights and broaden their horizons. Genuine curiosity goes beyond simply asking generic questions to show interest; it involves actively listening and seeking a deeper understanding of someone's experiences, perspectives, and opinions. When individuals approach conversations with an open mind and a sincere desire to learn from others, they can create a comfortable environment that encourages meaningful dialogue. This not only allows individuals to develop empathy and understanding but also encourages others to open up and share their thoughts more explicitly. Showing genuine curiosity about others can help individuals to break down barriers and bridge cultural differences, fostering a more inclusive and diverse community.

One way to demonstrate genuine curiosity is through active listening. It is important to be fully present during conversations, focusing on the speaker without distractions. By maintaining eye contact, nodding, and providing verbal cues, individuals can express their genuine interest in what the other person is saying. Asking open-ended questions that encourage further elaboration can convey a sense of curiosity and an eagerness to learn more. Genuine curiosity also involves seeking to understand the other person's perspectives and experiences, especially when they differ from one's own. By doing so, individuals can gain new insights, challenge their own beliefs, and foster personal growth. An important aspect of showing genuine curiosity is avoiding making assumptions or judgements about others. Each person has a unique background, experiences, and perspectives that contribute to who they are. It is crucial to approach conversations with an open mind and without preconceived notions. By asking questions that encourage individuals to delve deeper into their experiences and beliefs, a genuinely curious person can foster a safe and non-judgemental environment that allows others to feel comfortable sharing their thoughts and ideas.

Showing genuine curiosity about others extends beyond asking about their personal lives. It also involves showing interest in their passions, hobbies, and goals. By asking questions about someone's interests and actively engaging in conversations related to their passions, individuals can create stronger connections and deeper conversations. This curiosity can even lead to the discovery of shared interests, further strengthening the bond between individuals. Showing genuine curiosity about others is essential for being a good conversationalist. By actively listening, seeking to understand, avoiding assumptions, and showing interest in various aspects of someone's life, individuals can foster deeper connections and gain valuable insights. Genuine curiosity not only fosters empathy and understanding but also promotes inclusivity and diversity within communities. By embracing this curiosity, individuals can become better conversationalists and build stronger relationships with the people they encounter.

ASKING OPEN-ENDED QUESTIONS

Asking open-ended questions is a crucial skill to have when aiming to become a good conversationalist. Open-ended questions are those that require more than a simple yes or no answer and encourage the person being asked to provide a detailed response. These types of questions are valuable because they allow for deeper and more meaningful conversations to take place. By asking open-ended questions, one demonstrates an active interest in the thoughts and opinions of others, and this can lead to a greater level of engagement and connection within conversations. When someone is asked an open-ended question, they are given the opportunity to express themselves fully, which can foster a sense of validation and respect. For example, instead of asking, "Did you like the movie?" a better open-ended question could be, "What did you think of the movie and why?" This allows the person to provide a more nuanced response, sharing their specific thoughts and reasoning behind their opinion. Open-ended questions also serve as a way to inquire about someone's experiences, beliefs, or interests, allowing conversations to delve into a variety of topics and explore different perspectives. By asking questions that prompt further reflection and discussion, conversationalists can create a more enriching and engaging dialogue. Open-ended questions can contribute to the development of critical thinking skills, as they require individuals to think more deeply and articulate their thoughts more clearly. This not only benefits the person being asked, but it also enhances the overall conversational experience for both parties involved. Open-ended questions can help to foster active listening skills, as they encourage individuals to pay attention to the responses they receive and follow up with relevant queries. When one consistently asks open-ended questions, they demonstrate a genuine eagerness to learn and engage with others, which can have a positive impact on the overall quality of their conversations. It is important to note that using open-ended questions effectively requires practice and attentiveness. It is crucial to ask questions that are relevant and appropriate to the context of the conversation and to be genuinely interested in the responses given. When asking open-ended questions, it is also important to allow enough time for the person to answer and avoid interrupting their train of thought. By mastering the art of asking open-ended questions, individuals can create an environment that promotes open and thoughtful communication, facilitating the formation of stronger relationships and a deeper understanding of others. By incorporating open-ended questions into their conversational toolbox, one can become a more skilled and engaging conversationalist.

LISTENING ACTIVELY TO DEEPEN CONNECTIONS

Active listening is a skill that can greatly enhance our ability to connect with others in meaningful conversations. By listening actively, we show others that we value their thoughts and opinions, and we create a safe space for them to express themselves openly. To listen actively, we must be fully present in the conversation, both mentally and physically. This means putting away distractions such as our phones or laptops and focusing our attention on the person speaking. We can also use non-verbal cues, such as maintaining eye contact and nodding our head, to demonstrate that we are engaged in the conversation. Active listening involves asking clarifying questions and seeking to understand the speaker's perspective. By doing so, we show genuine interest in what they have to say and deepen our connection with them. Actively listening also involves resisting the urge to interrupt or interject our own thoughts and experiences. Instead, we allow the speaker to fully express themselves before offering our input. This not only shows respect for the speaker but also allows for a more balanced and equitable conversation. Another important aspect of active listening is paraphrasing or summarizing what the speaker has said to ensure that we have understood their message correctly. This not only helps to avoid misunderstandings but also shows the speaker that we are actively engaged in the conversation. By restating their ideas in our own words, we can also provide them with a sense of validation and affirmation. Active listening involves being aware of our own biases and judgments and setting them aside to be open to new perspectives. This can be challenging at times, especially if we hold strong beliefs or opinions on a particular topic. By being open-minded and willing to consider alternative viewpoints, we create a space for genuine dialogue and learning to take place. Active listening requires patience and empathy. We must be patient with the speaker, allowing them the time and space to fully express themselves. This may involve giving them encouragement or asking open-ended questions to help them delve deeper into their thoughts and feelings. Showing empathy towards the speaker by acknowledging their emotions and validating their experiences fosters a sense of trust and understanding. Active listening is a crucial skill for deepening connections in conversations. By being fully present, using non-verbal cues, asking clarifying questions, summarizing, setting aside biases, and practicing patience and empathy, we can create meaningful and rewarding connections with others. Embracing active listening not only enriches our own understanding but also demonstrates our commitment to building genuine and respectful relationships with those around us. Another important aspect of being a good conversationalist is the ability to actively listen. Many people underestimate the power of listening in a conversation, often focusing more on talking themselves. Active listening is crucial for a meaningful and engaging exchange. To be an active listener, one must not only pay attention but also show genuine interest in the speaker's words, thoughts, and emotions. This involves maintaining eye contact, nodding or making appropriate facial expressions to indicate understanding or empathy, and avoiding distractions or interruptions. By actively listening, one demonstrates respect towards the speaker and creates a safe space for sharing ideas and opinions without judgment. Active listening allows one to understand the speaker's perspective and grasp the underlying meanings conveyed through nonverbal cues. It enables the listener to ask relevant questions, clarify any uncertainties, and provide thoughtful responses that contribute to the conversation flow. Active listening promotes effective communication and fosters stronger connections between individuals. When we feel heard and understood, we are more inclined to open up and engage in deeper conversations. Consequently, active listening helps combat superficiality and allows for the exploration of more meaningful topics, forging stronger bonds and enriching our social interactions.

In addition to active listening, good conversationalists also possess the ability to empathize with others. Empathy is the capacity to understand and share the feelings of another person, and it plays a vital role in fostering connections and building rapport. By putting ourselves in someone else's shoes, we gain insight into their experiences and emotions, enabling us to respond compassionately and appropriately. Empathy helps create a supportive environment that encourages open communication and enables others to feel heard, validated, and understood. It allows us to respond not just with our words but also with our hearts, showing genuine care and concern for the person we are conversing with. Consequently, empathy leads to more authentic and engaging conversations, instilling a sense of trust and mutual respect. By practicing empathy, we cultivate a deeper understanding of the human experience and develop stronger relationships that extend beyond surface-level interactions.

Being a good conversationalist requires more than just the ability to speak coherently and express oneself effectively. It involves active listening and empathizing with others, essential skills that enable meaningful and engaging conversations. By actively listening, we demonstrate respect towards the speaker, understand their perspective, and contribute thoughtfully to the dialogue. Likewise, empathy allows us to connect on a deeper level, making the conversation more genuine and enriching. Together, active listening and empathy create a harmonious and supportive environment that fosters connection, understanding, and personal growth. Thus, mastering these skills is crucial for anyone seeking to become a good conversationalist and to build stronger, more meaningful relationships.

IX. CULTIVATING KNOWLEDGE AND CURIOSITY

Cultivating knowledge and curiosity is essential for becoming a good conversationalist. The foundation of engaging conversations lies in possessing a genuine thirst for knowledge and a genuine curiosity about the world. By actively seeking knowledge and keeping up with current events, one can engage in meaningful discussions with others. Reading books, newspapers, and articles, exploring different subjects, and maintaining an open mind are key elements in cultivating knowledge and curiosity. Firstly, reading is a fundamental activity for acquiring knowledge and broadening one's perspective. Engaging in various genres and types of literature can expose individuals to different ideas, cultures, and perspectives. By reading extensively, one can learn about different topics such as history, science, literature, and philosophy, which can enrich conversations and spark intellectual curiosity. Reading newspapers and articles is crucial for staying informed about current events, allowing individuals to contribute to discussions on relevant and pressing issues. Secondly, exploring different subjects and areas of interest is vital for cultivating knowledge and curiosity. By venturing beyond one's comfort zone and exploring unfamiliar territories, individuals can discover new passions and broaden their intellectual horizons. Participating in diverse activities, such as attending workshops, lectures, and cultural events, can enable individuals to learn from experts and artists firsthand. This exposure to various subjects not only nurtures curiosity but also equips individuals with knowledge that can be shared and discussed with others. Maintaining an open mind is essential for cultivating both knowledge and curiosity. Being receptive to different viewpoints, ideas, and experiences encourages individuals to challenge their own beliefs and expand their understanding. Through embracing intellectual diversity, individuals can engage in constructive debates and conversations that foster mutual learning and growth. Maintaining an open mind allows individuals to appreciate the uniqueness of others' perspectives, which in turn contributes to a more inclusive and engaging conversational environment. Becoming a good conversationalist entails cultivating knowledge and curiosity. By reading extensively, exploring different subjects, and maintaining an open mind, individuals can acquire knowledge, broaden their horizons, and engage in meaningful conversations with others. Cultivating knowledge and curiosity not only enriches conversations but also fosters personal growth and intellectual development. It enables individuals to contribute to discussions and debates with a well-rounded understanding of various topics, enhancing their ability to connect with others on a deeper level. The pursuit of knowledge and curiosity is an ongoing journey that not only enhances one's conversational skills but also enriches one's life as a whole.

STAYING INFORMED ABOUT VARIOUS SUBJECTS

Staying informed about various subjects is an essential skill for becoming a good conversationalist. In today's fast-paced world, where information is readily accessible at our fingertips, it has become increasingly important to keep oneself updated and informed about a wide range of topics. When engaging in a conversation, having knowledge about different subjects allows one to contribute meaningfully and actively participate in discussions. Firstly, staying informed allows individuals to stay on top of current events and be aware of the latest developments in society. This includes being updated on politics, economics, and other global issues that impact our daily lives. By having an understanding of these subjects, one can engage in conversations that delve into the complexities of the world, sharing informed opinions and insights. This not only demonstrates intellectual curiosity but also shows respect for the other person's perspective, fostering a deeper level of connection and mutual understanding. Being knowledgeable about a wide array of subjects enables individuals to have a more diverse range of conversations, making them more interesting and engaging communicators. By actively seeking out information and learning about different fields of study, individuals broaden their horizons and develop a well-rounded view of the world. This enables them to engage in conversations about art, literature, science, technology, sports, and other domains, thereby making them versatile conversationalists who can adapt to various social settings.

Staying informed about different subjects allows individuals to bring new insights and fresh perspectives to conversations. By reading extensively and delving deep into a particular subject, individuals acquire specialized knowledge that can spark intellectual debates and enrich their interactions with others. This not only makes conversations more engaging but also encourages others to actively contribute their own unique perspectives. Being knowledgeable about various subjects fosters a sense of confidence and self-assuredness, making individuals more comfortable in engaging in conversations. They become more willing to ask thoughtful questions and actively listen to others, leading to a more meaningful exchange of ideas. Staying informed about various subjects is a crucial aspect of becoming a good conversationalist. By staying updated on current events, having knowledge of different fields, and bringing fresh insights to discussions, individuals can engage meaningfully with others, fostering mutual understanding and connection. This not only enhances their own intellectual growth but also contributes to creating a vibrant and dynamic social environment. In a world where information is abundant, being armed with knowledge allows individuals to actively participate in conversations and make a lasting impression on those they engage with. Staying informed is not only about becoming a good conversationalist but also about developing a lifelong love for learning and expanding one's horizons.

READING DIVERSE MATERIALS

Reading diverse materials is an essential practice for individuals aiming to become good conversationalists. Engaging with a wide range of literary genres, styles, and perspectives allows individuals to expand their knowledge, broaden their horizons, and develop empathy towards others. By reading diverse materials, individuals are exposed to different cultures, experiences, and ideas, allowing them to gain a deep understanding and appreciation of the complexities of the world. This exposure fosters open-mindedness and helps individuals to challenge their own preconceived notions and biases. Reading diverse materials enhances one's ability to engage in meaningful conversations with people from various backgrounds. It equips individuals with a vast pool of knowledge and reference points, enabling them to connect with others on a deeper level. They can draw upon references from literature, history, or philosophy to contribute to discussions and offer unique insights. Reading diverse materials provides individuals with a variety of perspectives, which can help them become more critical thinkers. By encountering different viewpoints, they learn to evaluate arguments from various angles, strengthening their analytical skills. This enhances their ability to engage in debates and discussions, making their conversations more stimulating and intellectually engaging. Reading diverse materials cultivates empathy and compassion within individuals. By immersing themselves in the stories and experiences of characters from different walks of life, readers develop a nuanced understanding of human emotions, motivations, and struggles. This increased understanding allows individuals to relate to others more effectively, providing a solid foundation for meaningful conversations. It fosters a sense of empathy and compassion towards others, enabling individuals to engage in conversations with kindness, understanding, and respect. Reading diverse materials offers individuals an opportunity for self-reflection and personal growth. By encountering characters with diverse backgrounds and experiences, readers are prompted to reflect upon their own beliefs, values, and biases. This introspection allows individuals to identify areas for personal growth and development, leading to a greater level of self-awareness. Reading diverse materials can expose individuals to new ideas or perspectives that challenge their existing worldview, potentially leading to personal transformation. Reading diverse materials is a crucial practice for becoming a good conversationalist. It not only expands one's knowledge and understanding of the world but also enhances critical thinking skills, cultivates empathy and compassion, and promotes personal growth. By actively engaging with diverse literature, individuals equip themselves with a rich repertoire of knowledge and perspectives, enabling them to engage in meaningful conversations with people from various backgrounds. Reading diverse materials encourages individuals to challenge their own biases and preconceptions, fostering open-mindedness and facilitating intellectual growth. Individuals should embrace the practice of reading diverse materials as a means to develop into more effective and engaging conversationalists.

SEEKING OUT NEW EXPERIENCES AND PERSPECTIVES

In addition to actively listening and engaging in meaningful conversations, a good conversationalist is constantly seeking out new experiences and perspectives. By challenging oneself to step outside of their comfort zone and explore unfamiliar territories, one can broaden their horizons and gain a deeper understanding of the world around them. This entails making a conscious effort to seek out diverse viewpoints, whether it be through reading books from different genres or engaging in discussions with people from various cultures and backgrounds. By doing so, individuals can break free from the confines of their own personal biases and preconceived notions, opening themselves up to a wealth of new ideas and perspectives. Seeking out new experiences allows one to continually grow and evolve as an individual. One may discover hidden passions and interests that they never knew they had, or uncover new insights and wisdom that can enrich their lives. It also helps to foster a sense of empathy and understanding towards others, as they are able to see the world through a different lens, gaining a greater appreciation for the complexities and nuances of human experience. By actively seeking out new experiences and perspectives, a good conversationalist is able to draw on a rich tapestry of knowledge and understanding, making them more well-rounded and insightful in their interactions with others. Seeking out new experiences and perspectives also enables individuals to overcome their own limitations and biases. It challenges them to question their own assumptions and consider alternative viewpoints, helping them to grow intellectually and emotionally. This willingness to explore new terrain and embrace the unknown is not only vital in the realm of conversation, but also in all aspects of life. It allows individuals to adapt to new situations and navigate uncertain circumstances with confidence and resilience. By actively seeking out new experiences and perspectives, a good conversationalist is able to approach conversations with a sense of curiosity and openness, creating an environment that encourages dialogue and fosters mutual respect. Seeking out new experiences and perspectives is essential in becoming a good conversationalist. It not only broadens one's understanding of the world, but also challenges their own biases and limitations, fostering growth and empathy. By actively exploring unfamiliar territories, individuals can gain a wealth of knowledge and insights that enrich their interactions with others. This mindset of curiosity and openness enables individuals to navigate through life with confidence and resilience. It is crucial for individuals to continually seek out new experiences and perspectives in order to become skilled conversationalists, fostering meaningful connections and understanding with others.

CONTINUOUSLY LEARNING FROM OTHERS

In order to engage in meaningful and insightful discussions, it is essential to approach conversations with an open mind and a willingness to learn from others. This involves actively listening to the perspectives and experiences shared by individuals from diverse backgrounds, and being receptive to new ideas and concepts. By doing so, one can expand their knowledge and broaden their horizons, enabling them to engage in conversations on a wide range of topics. Learning from others encompasses more than just gaining knowledge. It also entails developing greater empathy and understanding towards different points of view. As individuals, we are shaped by our personal backgrounds, beliefs, and experiences. Consequently, our outlook may be limited or biased in certain situations. Engaging in conversations with others allows us to challenge our own perspectives and consider alternative viewpoints. By actively seeking out different opinions and understanding the rationale behind them, we can develop a more comprehensive understanding of the world around us. Learning from others involves acknowledging the expertise and experiences of individuals in specific fields. Conversations are an opportunity to tap into the vast pool of knowledge possessed by others. For instance, discussing a particular interest or hobby with an expert in that field can provide invaluable insights and deepen our understanding. By actively seeking advice or guidance from those who possess knowledge and experience, we can enhance our own understanding and make more informed decisions.

Continuous learning from others allows us to develop our own communication skills. Consciously observing how others articulate their thoughts and ideas, as well as their use of body language and tone, can provide valuable lessons in effective communication. Engaging in conversations with skilled communicators provides opportunities to learn from their techniques and implement them in our own discussions. This can ultimately improve our ability to convey our thoughts clearly, assertively, and diplomatically, fostering better connections and relationships with others. Continuously learning from others is a vital characteristic of a good conversationalist. It involves actively listening, staying open-minded, and seeking out diverse perspectives. By doing so, individuals can broaden their knowledge, develop empathy, and understand alternative viewpoints. Acknowledging the expertise of others enables one to tap into a wealth of knowledge and expand their understanding in different areas. Learning from others not only enhances our own knowledge and skills, but also enriches our interactions, fostering meaningful and engaging conversations that contribute to personal growth and development.

EXPANDING KNOWLEDGE BASE THROUGH CONVERSATIONS

Expanding knowledge base through conversations is a crucial skill that can greatly enhance one's personal and professional development. Engaging in meaningful conversations with others allows individuals to access a wealth of diverse and unique perspectives, ideas, and information that they might not have encountered otherwise. This exchange of knowledge not only broadens one's horizons but also promotes intellectual growth and critical thinking. Through conversations, we have the opportunity to explore different subjects, from history and politics to science and arts, and gain insights that enable us to see the world from various angles. Engaging in conversations with individuals from different backgrounds and cultures gives us the chance to appreciate and understand diverse viewpoints, fostering empathy and tolerance. This aspect of expanding knowledge base through conversations is particularly important in today's interconnected world, where cultural understanding and open-mindedness are highly valued. Conversations provide an avenue for individuals to stay up-to-date with the latest developments and trends in various fields. By actively participating in discussions, one can learn about new discoveries, innovations, and research findings, ultimately enriching their knowledge base and keeping them intellectually informed. Conversations allow us to challenge our own assumptions and beliefs, encouraging personal growth and development. When engaged in thoughtful dialogues, we are prompted to critically examine our own ideas, opinions, and biases, fostering an environment of intellectual growth and self-reflection. By exposing ourselves to alternative perspectives, we have the opportunity to refine our understanding of complex issues, becoming more well-rounded individuals in the process. Conversations provide a platform for knowledge-sharing, both in terms of personally acquired knowledge and information obtained from external sources. By sharing expertise and insights, individuals can contribute to the intellectual development of others, creating a positive feedback loop of knowledge expansion. This not only benefits the individuals involved but also promotes the advancement of society as a whole. Expanding knowledge base through conversations requires active participation, curiosity, and open-mindedness. Engaging in thoughtful and reflective discussions allows individuals to tap into a vast pool of knowledge and experiences, broadening their perspectives and deepening their understanding of the world. By actively seeking out opportunities to engage in meaningful conversations, individuals can nurture their intellectual curiosity and continue their personal and professional growth. Mastering the art of conversationalism is not only essential for effective communication but also a pathway to expanding knowledge and fostering intellectual development.

BEING OPEN TO NEW IDEAS AND INSIGHTS

Being open to new ideas and insights is an essential quality that a good conversationalist possesses. When engaging in a conversation, it is crucial to approach it with an open mind and a willingness to consider alternative perspectives. By being receptive to new ideas, individuals can broaden their knowledge and gain a deeper understanding of the world around them. Openness to new ideas also fosters intellectual growth and encourages personal development. An individual who is open to new insights recognizes that they do not have a monopoly on knowledge and that there is always more to learn. This humility allows them to engage in conversations with a genuine curiosity and a desire to expand their understanding. One of the major benefits of being open to new ideas and insights is that it promotes meaningful and stimulating conversations. When individuals approach a conversation with an open mind, they create an environment that encourages the exchange of ideas and the exploration of different perspectives. This, in turn, leads to more engaging and fulfilling discussions. By being open to new insights, individuals can challenge their own preconceived notions and expectations, allowing for a deeper analysis of their own beliefs and ideologies. This self-reflection promotes intellectual growth and expands one's ability to engage in meaningful conversations.

In addition, being open to new ideas and insights also facilitates personal growth and development. When individuals are receptive to new insights, they are able to expand their knowledge base and gain a more comprehensive understanding of the world. This not only enhances their intellectual abilities but also broadens their horizons, enabling them to view the world from different perspectives. This openness to new ideas fosters adaptability and flexibility, qualities that are highly valued in today's rapidly changing world. By being open to new insights, individuals can embrace change, overcome challenges, and navigate unfamiliar territories with ease.

Being open to new ideas and insights enables individuals to build stronger and more meaningful relationships. When engaging in conversations, individuals who are open to new insights demonstrate respect and attentiveness towards others' opinions and ideas. This fosters a sense of mutual understanding and creates a safe space for open and honest conversations. By actively listening and considering alternative viewpoints, individuals can form deeper connections with others and foster a sense of empathy and understanding. This open-mindedness contributes to the creation of a supportive and inclusive conversational environment, where all participants feel valued and heard.

To conclude, being open to new ideas and insights is a crucial quality for being a good conversationalist. It promotes intellectual growth, stimulates meaningful conversations, and enhances personal development. By embracing new insights and alternative perspectives, individuals can broaden their knowledge, challenge their beliefs, and develop a deeper understanding of the world. This openness to new ideas not only facilitates personal growth but also fosters more meaningful connections with others. By cultivating an open mind and a willingness to consider new insights, individuals can become better conversationalists and enrich their lives in countless ways.

To be a good conversationalist, one must possess certain qualities and hone specific skills that allow for meaningful and engaging interactions with others. Firstly, a good conversationalist is someone who actively listens. This entails being fully present in the conversation and showing genuine interest in what the other person is saying. Rather than waiting for their turn to speak or letting their mind wander, a good conversationalist focuses on the speaker's words, body language, and emotions, providing them with their undivided attention. A good conversationalist is capable of empathizing with others. This involves understanding and acknowledging the speaker's feelings and perspective, even if they differ from their own. By showing empathy, a good conversationalist fosters a safe and non-judgmental environment where the speaker feels heard and understood. Another important quality of a good conversationalist is the ability to ask thought-provoking questions. By asking open-ended questions, a good conversationalist encourages the speaker to delve deeper into their thoughts and emotions, leading to more meaningful exchanges. A good conversationalist actively contributes to the conversation by sharing personal experiences, insights, or relevant information. By offering their own perspectives, thoughts, and expertise, a good conversationalist adds depth and value to the discussion, keeping it engaging and substantive. In addition to these qualities, a good conversationalist also possesses the skill of effective communication. They are able to convey their ideas and thoughts clearly and articulately, using appropriate language and tone. This skill allows a good conversationalist to express themselves in a way that is easily understood and can be appreciated by others. A good conversationalist is knowledgeable and well-informed about a wide range of topics. This allows them to contribute meaning-fully to conversations, bringing in different perspectives and insights that enrich the dialogue. A good conversationalist is aware of non-verbal cues and understands the importance of body language in communication. They pay attention to their own body language, ensuring it aligns with their words and intentions. A good conversationalist is observant of the other person's body language, allowing them to pick up on subtle cues such as facial expressions and gestures, and adapt their approach accordingly. A good conversationalist is respectful of others' opinions and beliefs. They understand that conversations are not about winning arguments or proving oneself right but rather about sharing and exchanging ideas. By maintaining respect for differing opinions, a good conversationalist fosters a sense of inclusivity and openness, creating an environment conducive to constructive dialogue. Being a good conversationalist requires a combination of qualities and skills that facilitate meaningful, engaging, and respectful interactions. Actively listening, empathizing, asking thought-provoking questions, sharing personal experiences, and being knowledgeable about various topics are some of the qualities necessary to excel in this skill. Effective communication, awareness of non-verbal cues, and respect for others' opinions are vital in creating an environment that encourages open and fruitful discussion.

X. BEING MINDFUL OF NON-VERBAL FEEDBACK

In addition to actively listening and responding appropriately to verbal cues, being mindful of non-verbal feedback is crucial to becoming a good conversationalist. Non-verbal communication encompasses various aspects, including body language, facial expressions, and tone of voice. While words convey the explicit message, non-verbal cues often reveal the underlying emotions and attitudes of an individual. Understanding and interpreting these non-verbal signals can significantly enhance the effectiveness of communication, leading to more meaningful and engaging conversations. One significant element of non-verbal communication is body language, which can provide invaluable insights into a person's thoughts and feelings. For instance, crossed arms or hands on hips may indicate defensiveness or hostility, while leaning forward and maintaining eye contact often conveys attentiveness and interest. Mirroring the body language of a speaker can foster a sense of connection and rapport, indicating an openness to what they are saying. Being mindful of one's own body language is equally important. Maintaining an open posture and using appropriate gestures can signal attentiveness, understanding, and respect towards the speaker, thus encouraging them to feel more comfortable in engaging in conversation. Facial expressions also play a significant role in non-verbal communication. A smile can convey warmth, friendliness, and positive engagement in a conversation, fostering a welcoming atmosphere. On the other hand, a furrowed brow or a frown may indicate confusion, disagreement, or disinterest. Being mindful of these facial expressions, both on the part of the listener and the speaker, allows for more accurate interpretations of the emotional context of a conversation, facilitating better understanding and connection between individuals.

Tone of voice can significantly impact the message being conveyed. The way words are spoken, including volume, pitch, and intonation, can influence how the listener perceives and interprets the conversation. An enthusiastic tone can convey excitement and passion, while a monotonous or aggressive tone may undermine the overall message. Being attentive to changes in tone can help to understand and respond accordingly to the emotional state of the speaker, further demonstrating empathy and active engagement in the conversation.

Being mindful of non-verbal feedback is an essential aspect of effective communication and being a good conversationalist. By paying attention to body language, facial expressions, and tone of voice, individuals can gain deeper insights into the emotions, attitudes, and intentions behind the words being exchanged. This knowledge allows for more accurate interpretations, fostering better understanding and connection between individuals. Developing the ability to observe and interpret non-verbal cues contributes to the overall effectiveness of communication, leading to more meaningful and engaging conversations. Mastering the art of non-verbal communication is a valuable skill that can enhance one's conversational abilities and ultimately improve interpersonal relationships.

PAYING ATTENTION TO CUES FROM OTHERS

In the realm of effective communication, paying attention to cues from others plays a crucial role in becoming a skilled conversationalist. Cues from others, whether they are verbal or nonverbal, provide valuable information about their thoughts, feelings, and reactions, enabling us to adapt and adjust our communication style accordingly. Verbally, cues manifest in the form of direct statements, questions, or opinions expressed during a conversation. These cues can be as simple as an exclamation of agreement or disagreement, indicating the listener's level of engagement and understanding. By actively listening to and acknowledging these verbal cues, we demonstrate that we value the other person's input and perspectives, fostering a sense of respect and validation. Paying attention to the cues enables us to guide the conversation, keeping it focused and relevant. On the other hand, nonverbal cues, such as body language, facial expressions, and tone of voice, can reveal a multitude of information about the speaker's emotional state, level of comfort, or agreement. For instance, crossed arms might indicate defensiveness or disinterest, while maintaining eye contact suggests attentiveness and engagement. Noticing these nonverbal cues allows us to gauge the speaker's comfort level and adjust our communication style to create a more welcoming and inclusive environment. Being attuned to nonverbal cues helps us understand the underlying emotions behind the words spoken. For instance, a hesitant tone or a furrowed brow might suggest that the speaker is unsure or concerned, prompting us to offer support or clarification. Importantly, responding to both verbal and nonverbal cues allows the conversation to flow more smoothly and creates a sense of mutual understanding and connection. Paying attention to cues from others not only enhances our conversational skills but also strengthens our ability to empathize and build meaningful relationships. By actively listening and responding to cues, we show a genuine interest in the other person and their views, establishing a foundation of trust and respect. This receptiveness also promotes a safe space for sharing diverse ideas and perspectives, vital in cultivating a culture of inclusivity and acceptance. In addition, understanding and responding to cues from others also allows us to adapt our communication style to varying social contexts. For instance, in a formal setting, such as a job interview, recognizing cues for professionalism and maintaining a respectful tone can contribute to a positive impression. Alternatively, in more casual settings, picking up on cues for humor or relaxation can create a relaxed and comfortable atmosphere, conducive to open conversation. Being attentive to cues from others is an indispensable skill for anyone aspiring to be a good conversationalist. Verbal and nonverbal cues provide valuable insight into the thoughts, emotions, and reactions of the speaker, ensuring that our communication is respectful, relevant, and engaging. By actively listening and responding to cues, we foster a sense of connection, empathy, and understanding, allowing us to build meaningful relationships and navigate various social contexts with ease. By paying attention to cues from others, we can elevate our conversational skills and enrich our interactions with others.

RECOGNIZING SIGNS OF DISCOMFORT OR DISENGAGEMENT

Recognizing signs of discomfort or disengagement is crucial in maintaining effective and engaging conversations. People may exhibit various nonverbal and verbal cues that indicate their disinterest or discomfort during a conversation. Nonverbal signs can include avoiding eye contact, crossing arms, fidgeting, or leaning away. These actions often suggest a disengagement from the conversation and a desire to withdraw. On the other hand, verbal cues such as one-word answers, monotonous tone, or repeated change of subject may also indicate discomfort or disinterest. When conversing with others, it is essential to stay attuned to these signs, as they offer valuable insights into the other person's state of mind. Recognizing signs of discomfort or disengagement can be vital for several reasons. Firstly, it helps to establish a positive and respectful atmosphere during a conversation. By being attentive to the signals of discomfort, we demonstrate our empathy and understanding towards the other person. This can foster a sense of trust and openness, allowing for a more meaningful and genuine exchange of ideas. Recognizing these signs can help avoid miscommunication or misunderstanding. If one party is feeling uncomfortable or disengaged, it is likely that they are not fully comprehending or processing the information being conveyed. By noticing and addressing these signs promptly, we can ensure that all participants are on the same page, enhancing the overall effectiveness of the conversation. Recognizing signs of discomfort or disengagement can provide an opportunity to adjust the flow and content of the conversation. If someone appears disinterested or uneasy, it may be helpful to redirect the discussion to a topic that they find more engaging or relevant. By doing so, we can create an environment where all participants feel included and valued, which can lead to more dynamic and fruitful exchanges. Acknowledging signs of discomfort may also prompt us to inquire about the other person's well-being or concerns. By actively demonstrating our concern for their comfort, we create a space for open and honest dialogue, thereby strengthening the quality of the conversation and the relationship with our interlocutor.

Recognizing signs of discomfort or disengagement is not only crucial for the quality of the conversation but also for our own growth as conversationalists. By being observant and responsive to the reactions of others, we can gain valuable insight into our own communication skills and areas for improvement. Recognizing when our conversational approach might be causing discomfort or disinterest allows us to adapt and refine our techniques, ultimately making us more effective and engaging conversationalists in the future. Recognizing signs of discomfort or disengagement is essential for maintaining effective and engaging conversations. By being attentive to nonverbal and verbal cues, we can establish a positive atmosphere, avoid miscommunication, adapt the conversation's flow, and foster personal growth. Being sensitive to these signs demonstrates our empathy, enhances the quality of the conversation, and strengthens our relationships with others.

ADJUSTING COMMUNICATION APPROACH ACCORDINGLY

In order to be a good conversationalist, one must know how to adjust their communication approach accordingly. This ability to adapt is crucial as every person we interact with is unique, and what may work for one individual may not work for another. One important aspect of adjusting our communication approach is considering the cultural background of the person we are conversing with. Different cultures have distinct communication styles and norms, and being aware of these can help avoid misunderstandings or unintended offense. For example, in some cultures, direct communication and expressing opinions openly may be valued, while in others, indirect communication and avoiding confrontation may be the norm. By being mindful of these differences, we can tailor our approach to fit the preferences of the person we are speaking with, thus establishing a more comfortable and effective conversation. Adjusting our communication approach also involves recognizing and accommodating individual communication preferences. Some people may prefer a more formal and structured conversation, while others may enjoy a more casual and free-flowing dialogue. It is important to gauge the communicative style of the person we are conversing with and adapt our approach accordingly. This could mean using more formal language and avoiding slang or jargon if the situation calls for it, or adopting a more relaxed and informal tone if the person seems more at ease in such a setting. By being flexible in our communication style, we create an environment that is conducive to open and respectful dialogue.

Another crucial aspect of adjusting our communication approach is listening actively and empathetically. Good conversationalists understand that communication is a two-way street, and that listening attentively is just as important as speaking. People appreciate being heard and understood, and by actively engaging in the conversation and demonstrating genuine interest, we not only create a positive and meaningful exchange but also build rapport with the person we are speaking with. Active listening involves maintaining eye contact, nodding, and providing verbal and non-verbal cues to indicate our understanding and engagement. By doing so, we show respect and appreciation for the speaker's perspective, promoting a more equal and inclusive conversation. Being a good conversationalist requires the ability to adjust our communication approach accordingly. This entails being mindful of cultural differences, recognizing and accommodating individual communication preferences, and actively listening and empathizing with the person we are conversing with. By adapting our approach to fit the needs and preferences of others, we create an environment that is conducive to meaningful and fruitful conversations. Being flexible in communication allows for better understanding, stronger connections, and More enjoyable and productive interactions.

REFLECTING ON ONE'S OWN NON-VERBAL COMMUNICATION

Non-verbal communication plays a crucial role in conveying our thoughts, emotions, and intentions to others. It includes body language, facial expressions, gestures, and tone of voice. Being aware of our non-verbal cues and reflecting on their impact is essential to effective communication. One way to reflect on our non-verbal communication is by observing ourselves in different social situations. We can pay attention to how we use our body, where we direct our gaze, and how we modulate our voice. For example, we might notice that we tend to cross our arms when we feel defensive or uncomfortable, or that we avoid eye contact when we are being dishonest. Reflecting on these observations allows us to identify patterns and tendencies that may hinder our communication skills. Reflecting on our non-verbal communication allows us to align our actions with our words. It is important to ensure that our non-verbal cues are congruent with the message we are trying to convey. For instance, if we are telling someone that we are excited about a particular topic, but our facial expression and body language convey boredom or disinterest, the other person might not take our words seriously. By becoming aware of these incongruencies through reflection, we can make conscious efforts to align our verbal and non-verbal communication, thereby increasing the effectiveness of our interactions. Another way to reflect on our non-verbal communication is by seeking feedback from others. We can ask trusted friends, family members, or mentors to observe our non-verbal cues and provide constructive feedback. This external perspective can offer valuable insights that we may not have noticed ourselves. Feedback allows us to identify any misinterpretations or misunderstandings that may have arisen due to our non-verbal cues. For example, someone might have perceived our crossed arms as a sign of defensiveness when, in reality, we were simply cold. By addressing these misunderstandings, we can mitigate potential conflicts and improve our overall communication skills. Reflecting on our own non-verbal communication also involves acknowledging cultural differences and adapting our cues accordingly. Different cultures have varying norms and expectations regarding non-verbal behavior. For example, in some cultures, direct eye contact is seen as a sign of respect, while in others, it may be perceived as confrontational. Reflecting on these cultural nuances can help us tailor our non-verbal cues to the specific context, ensuring that our message is received and understood effectively. Reflecting on one's own non-verbal communication is an indispensable component of becoming a good conversationalist. By observing ourselves and seeking feedback from others, we can identify patterns, incongruencies, and cultural differences in our non-verbal cues. This reflective process allows us to align our verbal and non-verbal communication, resolve misunderstandings, and adapt to different cultural contexts. Possessing a high level of self-awareness regarding our non-verbal communication enhances our overall communication skills and fosters meaningful and successful conversations.

EVALUATING UNINTENDED SIGNALS SENT TO OTHERS

Evaluating unintended signals sent to others is crucial in becoming a good conversationalist. In today's interconnected world, communication extends far beyond verbal exchanges. Nonverbal cues such as body language, facial expressions, and tone of voice play a significant role in conveying meaning and intent during conversations. It is not uncommon for individuals to inadvertently send unintended signals that can affect the outcome of a conversation. Understanding and evaluating these signals is essential for effective communication and building meaningful connections with others. Nonverbal cues, often referred to as the "silent language of communication", can reveal a person's true feelings and attitudes. For instance, a slight frown or crossed arms may inadvertently convey a sense of disagreement or disapproval, even if the words spoken remain positive. Such unintended signals can lead to misunderstandings and affect the overall progress of a conversation. Being attuned to nonverbal signals and evaluating them is vital to ensure that our intended message aligns with the signals we are sending.

One aspect of nonverbal communication that requires careful evaluation is body language. This includes gestures, postures, and facial expressions, all of which can significantly impact the perception of a conversation. For example, maintaining eye contact demonstrates active listening and interest, while avoiding eye contact may indicate disinterest or discomfort. Small gestures such as nodding or leaning in can signal attentiveness and engagement. By consistently evaluating our body language, we

can ensure that the nonverbal cues we are sending are congruent with our intended message, enhancing the overall quality of
our conversations. Another nonverbal cue that can inadvertently
affect a conversation is tone of voice. The way we speak, including our pitch, volume, and rhythm, can convey emotions, intentions, and attitudes. Different tones can be misinterpreted by
others, leading to confusion or misunderstandings. It is essential
to evaluate our tonal cues and ensure they align with the message we want to convey. By doing so, we can avoid sending
unintended signals that may hinder effective communication.
Evaluating unintended signals sent to others is an essential skill
in becoming a good conversationalist. Nonverbal cues, such as
body language and tone of voice, can often convey unintended
messages, risking the overall success of a conversation. By understanding and evaluating these signals, we can ensure that
our intended message aligns with the cues we are sending. By
being attuned to nonverbal communication, we can enhance effective communication, build meaningful connections, and ultimately become better conversationalists. It is crucial to continuously evaluate our nonverbal cues to be mindful of the signals
we may be sending to others.

MAKING NECESSARY ADJUSTMENTS TO FOSTER EFFECTIVE CONVERSATIONS

Being a good conversationalist requires more than just speaking and listening. It also involves making necessary adjustments to foster effective conversations. One important adjustment is being mindful of the tone and pace of the conversation. Different people have different preferences when it comes to the speed of communication. Some individuals prefer a fast-paced conversation while others might find it overwhelming. Similarly, the tone of the conversation sets the mood and can greatly affect how engaged and comfortable participants feel. It is crucial to gauge the preferences of the person you are conversing with to ensure a harmonious flow of dialogue. Being aware of non-verbal cues and body language is essential for effective communication. Non-verbal cues such as facial expressions, gestures, and posture can reveal a lot about a person's emotions and level of engagement. By paying attention to these cues, a good conversationalist can adjust their approach accordingly. For instance, if someone appears disinterested or uncomfortable, it may be necessary to change topics or try a different conversational style to keep them engaged. Flexibility is key in fostering effective conversations. Another adjustment that can contribute to productive dialogues is being an active listener. Active listening involves fully focusing on the speaker, showing genuine interest, and providing appropriate responses. This can be achieved by avoiding distractions and actively participating in the conversation. Asking clarifying questions, paraphrasing the speaker's points, and summarizing the discussion help to show understanding and foster a deeper level of engagement. It is also important to give the speaker enough time and space to express themselves without interrupting or dominating the conversation. This shows respect and allows for a more balanced exchange of ideas. Being aware of cultural differences is crucial in fostering effective conversations. Cultural norms, values, and communication styles vary across different societies and can greatly influence how conversations unfold. A good conversationalist recognizes and respects these differences, avoiding assumptions and stereotypes. They take the time to understand and appreciate diverse perspectives, creating an inclusive and welcoming atmosphere for everyone involved. Fostering effective conversations also requires managing conflicts or disagreements constructively. Disagreements are a natural part of any conversation, but how they are handled can determine the outcome and quality of the dialogue. Instead of resorting to aggression or defensiveness, a good conversationalist seeks common ground and focuses on problem-solving. They actively listen to opposing viewpoints, acknowledge valid concerns, and strive for mutual understanding. By maintaining a calm and respectful demeanor, it becomes easier to find solutions and build stronger connections with others. Making necessary adjustments to foster effective conversations is a vital skill for being a good conversationalist. This includes being mindful of the tone and pace of the conversation, paying attention to non-verbal cues, actively listening, respecting cultural differences, and managing conflicts constructively. By honing these skills, one can create meaningful and engaging dialogues that lead to deeper connections and richer exchanges of ideas. The art of active listening is a crucial component of being a good conversationalist. Active listening is a communication skill that involves fully engaging with and understanding the speaker's message. When engaging in a conversation, it is important to give the speaker your undivided attention and show genuine interest in what they are saying. This can be achieved by maintaining eye contact, nodding or using other nonverbal cues to show that you are actively listening. In addition, it is vital to avoid interrupting the speaker or formulating a response in your mind while they are still talking. Instead, allow them to fully express their thoughts before you respond. Active listening also involves asking relevant questions and seeking clarification to demonstrate your desire to understand their perspective. This not only shows respect for the speaker but also helps to deepen the conversation and foster mutual understanding. Paraphrasing or summarizing the speaker's points can further indicate that you are actively listening and comprehending their message. By restating their ideas in your own words, you can clarify any confusion and offer affirmation to the speaker. Showing empathy towards the speaker's emotions or experiences is essential in maintaining a meaningful conversation. Reflecting the speaker's emotions and expressing understanding or sympathy can create a supportive and open atmosphere, encouraging them to share more. It is vital to avoid judgment or criticism during the conversation as this can hinder the flow of a meaningful exchange. Instead, focus on understanding the speaker's perspective, even if you may not agree with it. Developing and maintaining good eye contact throughout the conversation is another crucial aspect of active listening. Eye contact demonstrates your focus and interest in the speaker, making them feel heard and valued. It is important to be mindful of cultural differences, as some cultures may view direct eye contact differently. Being patient is indispensable in becoming a good conversationalist. Conversations can often take unexpected turns, and it is important to remain patient and adapt to the flow of the dialogue. This means avoiding rushing the speaker or abruptly shifting the topic to suit your own interests. By allowing conversations to unfold naturally, you can foster genuine connections and create a comfortable environment for both parties to freely express themselves. Active listening is an indispensable skill for becoming a good conversationalist. By fully engaging with the speaker, maintaining eye contact, asking relevant questions, showing empathy, and being patient, one can create an environment that promotes meaningful conversation. Active listening not only helps to deepen understanding but also fosters connections and enriches relationships. Mastering active listening is vital for anyone looking to improve their conversational skills.

XI. MANAGING CONVERSATIONAL FLOW

Managing the flow of conversation is a crucial skill to master if one wishes to become a good conversationalist. Conversations can easily become disjointed and confusing if not properly guided by the participants. One effective way to manage conversational flow is by using transition phrases. Transition phrases, such as "on the other hand", "in addition", or "however", help to smoothly transition from one topic to another. By using these phrases, speakers can keep the conversation flowing and ensure that each participant has the opportunity to contribute to the discussion. It is important for a good conversationalist to be an active listener. Active listening involves giving one's full attention to the speaker and responding in a way that shows understanding and engagement. This can be accomplished through using appropriate body language, such as maintaining eye contact and nodding in agreement. A good conversationalist should be aware of nonverbal cues that indicate when someone wants to speak or has something to add to the conversation. It is important to allow others to interrupt or interject their thoughts when they feel the need to do so. Interrupting can be done politely by using phrases such as "if I may interject" or "excuse me for interrupting". By acknowledging and respecting these cues, the conversational flow can be effectively managed and all participants can feel included and valued.

Another aspect of managing conversational flow is the ability to redirect or steer the conversation when necessary. In some cases, the conversation may veer off-topic or become heated. A good conversationalist knows how to gently guide the discussion back on track or defuse potential conflicts. This can be achieved through asking open-ended questions that encourage the speaker to elaborate on their thoughts or by summarizing key points to refocus the conversation. Being cognizant of differing opinions and perspectives is essential in managing conversational flow. It is crucial to create an inclusive and safe space where everyone feels comfortable expressing their ideas and beliefs. A good conversationalist should never dismiss or invalidate someone's viewpoint but rather listen and seek to understand their perspective. Through active engagement and empathetic listening, a good conversationalist can navigate disagreements and foster a healthy and respectful discourse.

Managing conversational flow is a fundamental skill for being a good conversationalist. By using transition phrases, actively listening, and responding to nonverbal cues, the flow of conversation can be effectively managed, allowing for all participants to contribute to the discussion. The ability to redirect the conversation and create a safe space for diverse opinions is crucial in maintaining a fruitful dialogue. With practice and Mindfulness, anyone can become a skilled conversationalist, capable of engaging in meaningful and enriching conversations.

BALANCING TALKING AND LISTENING

Oftentimes, when engaged in a conversation, individuals tend to focus more on the talking aspect rather than listening attentively to the other person. To truly connect with others, it is necessary to strike a balance between talking and listening. First and foremost, effective communication involves active listening. When one genuinely listens to what the other person is saying, it shows respect and interest in their thoughts and opinions. Active listening entails focusing on the speaker's words, maintaining eye contact, and providing verbal and nonverbal cues to show that one is engaged in the conversation. By actively listening, individuals can gain a deeper understanding of the speaker's perspective and develop meaningful connections. Certain conversational situations call for a higher degree of listening rather than talking. For instance, when someone is seeking advice or sharing a personal experience, it is crucial to prioritize listening over talking. In such moments, people generally look for someone who can offer a listening ear and provide empathetic support. By allowing the other person to express themselves fully without interruption, a good conversationalist not only encourages emotional catharsis but also creates a safe space for open dialogue and understanding. On the other hand, while listening is essential, one must also contribute to the conversation by sharing their thoughts and opinions. Taking an active role in the conversation demonstrates assertiveness and engagement. Actively participating in a conversation fosters a sense of mutual respect between individuals. When both parties have the opportunity to speak and be heard, the conversation becomes balanced and dynamic. Sharing personal stories, experiences, or knowledge can enhance the overall quality of the conversation, as it adds depth and new perspectives. Although it is important to share one's thoughts, being aware of the amount of talking done and not overpowering the conversation is equally crucial. Conversations should not be one-sided monologues but rather interconnected exchanges between participants. When one person dominates the conversation, it not only diminishes the other person's engagement but also limits the flow of ideas and hinder the overall conversational experience. Mastering the art of balancing talking and listening is vital for becoming a good conversationalist. Active listening is the foundation upon which a real connection can be built, as it shows respect and interest in the other person. Knowing when to prioritize listening and when to contribute to the conversation is key in creating a balanced and engaging dialogue. By practicing this skill, individuals can foster meaningful connections, gain new perspectives, and enhance their communication abilities. Thus, achieving a balance between talking and listening is crucial for anyone seeking to become a skilled conversationalist.

AVOIDING EXCESSIVE TALKING OR DOMINATING THE CONVERSATION

Another crucial aspect of being a good conversationalist is avoiding excessive talking or dominating the conversation. Engaging in a dialogue involves actively listening and allowing others to express their thoughts and viewpoints. It is a common pitfall for some individuals to dominate the conversation by monopolizing the speaking time. This not only stifles the flow of the discussion but also hinders the development of a meaningful exchange of ideas. In order to avoid this, it is important to practice active listening skills and be mindful of one's own speaking time. A good conversationalist recognizes that a conversation should be a balanced and reciprocal interaction, where each participant has the opportunity to voice their opinions and thoughts. In order to achieve this equilibrium, one must resist the temptation to constantly interject or cut off others when they are speaking. Instead, it is crucial to let the speaker finish their thoughts before providing a response or asking clarifying questions. Interrupting others can give off the impression of disrespect or disinterest in their contributions to the conversation, thereby hindering the establishment of a positive rapport. Dominating the conversation often stems from a need to assert oneself or showcase intellectual superiority. A good conversationalist understands the value of humility and the importance of holding space for others to express themselves. By allowing others to have their fair share of speaking time, a conversationalist demonstrates respect for different perspectives, fosters a collaborative atmosphere, and creates an environment where everyone feels heard and valued.

It is important to recognize that listening, rather than talking, can often be the key to effective communication. When one is solely focused on their own voice, they miss out on the opportunity to gain new insights, deepen their understanding of various topics, and foster connections with others by empathizing with their experiences. In essence, excessive talking or dominating the conversation can hinder the richness and depth of an exchange. Practicing active listening and being mindful of one's speaking time are essential skills for becoming a good conversationalist. By doing so, individuals can create a space where ideas can be shared freely, diverse perspectives can be appreciated, and mutual understanding can be nurtured. This leads to more meaningful connections, enhanced interpersonal relationships, and a richer exchange of knowledge and experiences.

ENCOURAGING EQUAL PARTICIPATION

Encouraging equal participation is a crucial aspect of being a good conversationalist. In any conversation, it is essential to create an environment that fosters the active engagement of all participants. By encouraging equal participation, individuals feel valued, heard, and respected, leading to a more inclusive and meaningful conversation. To achieve this, a good conversationalist must be mindful of various factors. Firstly, one should ensure that everyone has an equal opportunity to speak. This requires actively listening and being aware of each participant's desire to contribute to the discussion. By giving everyone an equal chance to express their thoughts, ideas, and experiences, a good conversationalist can maximize the potential for meaningful dialogue. Secondly, it is important to validate and acknowledge each person's contributions. When individuals feel that their thoughts are appreciated, they are more likely to actively participate and share their perspective. Validating others' contributions can be achieved through positive reinforcement, such as nodding, affirming statements, or expressing interest in their ideas. This not only encourages equal participation but also enhances the overall quality of the conversation, as diverse perspectives are brought to the forefront. A good conversationalist should be mindful of the dynamics within the conversation. This includes being attentive to power imbalances and ensuring that all participants have an equal chance to contribute. By actively addressing and redistributing power, a good conversationalist can create an environment where everyone feels comfortable and empowered to speak up. Encouraging equal participation involves actively involving quieter participants who may be less inclined to share their thoughts. By actively seeking their input, asking open-ended questions, and providing them with opportunities to express themselves, a good conversationalist can ensure that all voices are heard. A good conversationalist should establish and enforce respectful communication norms. This includes encouraging active listening, empathy, and open-mindedness among participants. By setting the tone for respectful communication, a good conversationalist can create an atmosphere that supports equal participation. A good conversationalist should be aware of and challenge any biases or prejudices that may hinder equal participation. This requires self-reflection and continuous improvement to ensure that everyone feels valued and included in the conversation. Encouraging equal participation is essential for being a good conversationalist. By creating an environment that fosters active engagement, validating contributions, addressing power dynamics, involving quieter participants, establishing respectful communication norms, and challenging biases, a good conversationalist can maximize the potential for meaningful dialogue. Equal participation not only promotes inclusivity but also enriches the conversation by bringing diverse perspectives to the forefront. As society becomes more diverse, possessing the skills to encourage equal participation is increasingly valuable, as it allows for a deeper understanding of different perspectives and fosters unity and empathy among participants.

NAVIGATING BETWEEN TOPICS SMOOTHLY

Navigating between topics smoothly is a fundamental skill for being a good conversationalist. It entails the ability to transition seamlessly from one subject to another while keeping the flow and energy of the conversation intact. One key aspect of this skill is being attentive to the other person and picking up on cues that indicate their level of interest or engagement. Paying close attention to their body language, facial expressions, and verbal responses can help determine whether they are invested in the current topic or if it might be time to move on. It is important to gauge the depth of the conversation and adjust accordingly. Shallow topics may require quicker transitions, while deep and meaningful discussions may benefit from more gradual transitions. Another strategy for smooth topic navigation is to employ bridging techniques. These techniques involve making connections between different subjects, finding common ground, or identifying related themes. By finding threads that connect two seemingly unrelated topics, a conversationalist can create a seamless transition that keeps the conversation flowing naturally. For instance, if the conversation is about technology and someone brings up a recent camping trip, the conversationalist can bridge the gap by discussing how technology has influenced camping experiences or by exploring the technology used in outdoor activities. In addition to the aforementioned strategies, maintaining an open mind and being knowledgeable about a wide range of subjects can greatly enhance the ability to navigate between topics. An open mind allows for genuine curiosity and interest in the other person's experiences, enabling the conversation to evolve organically. Being well-informed about various topics, whether through reading, staying up to date with current events, or engaging in diverse experiences, provides conversationalists with a wealth of knowledge to draw upon. This knowledge allows them to contribute meaningful insights, ask thoughtful questions, and explore new avenues within the conversation. Despite the importance of smooth topic navigation, it is essential to strike a balance between keeping the conversation engaging and not overwhelming the other person. Jumping from topic to topic haphazardly can be disorienting and make it difficult for the other person to follow or contribute. It is crucial to be mindful of the pace and rhythm of the conversation, allowing for natural pauses and moments of reflection. This way, both parties can fully participate and feel valued in the exchange of ideas. Navigating between topics smoothly is a crucial skill for being a good conversationalist. Being attentive to the other person, utilizing bridging techniques, maintaining an open mind, and being knowledgeable about various subjects all contribute to seamless transitions and a vibrant conversation. Striking a balance between maintaining engagement and not overwhelming the other person is key. By honing these skills, one can become a skilled conversationalist capable of orchestrating engaging and meaningful discussions.

TRANSITIONING NATURALLY BETWEEN RELATED SUBJECTS

Transitioning naturally between related subjects is a vital skill for a good conversationalist. This ability allows individuals to flow effortlessly from one topic to another, maintaining the momentum and engagement in a conversation. One effective strategy for transitioning between related subjects is through the use of bridging statements or questions. For instance, when discussing a particular topic such as art, one could smoothly transition to a related subject such as literature by saying, "Speaking of creative expressions, have you read any interesting books lately?" This technique not only connects the two topics but also demonstrates active listening and genuine interest in the conversation. The use of shared experiences or commonalities between subjects can facilitate seamless transitions. By identifying overlapping themes or concepts, one can smoothly shift the focus of the conversation without abruptly changing the subject. For instance, if discussing an upcoming vacation and mentioning the beauty of natural landscapes, a conversationalist may transition to a related subject such as environmental conservation by stating, "It's amazing how diverse our planet is. Did you know that there are several organizations dedicated to preserving these natural wonders?" This approach helps bridge the gap between subjects, maintaining the relevance and coherence of the conversation. Acknowledging and building upon previous remarks can facilitate smooth transitions. By referencing earlier points or statements, a conversationalist can smoothly move from one related subject to another. This technique not only demonstrates active listening but also creates a sense of continuity in the conversation. For instance, if discussing the benefits of outdoor activities, one could transition to a related subject of physical fitness by saying, "You mentioned earlier how hiking helps you stay active. Have you tried any other activities that promote a healthy lifestyle?" This approach allows for a seamless shift between subjects while keeping the conversation dynamic and engaging. In addition to these strategies, non-verbal cues such as body language and intonation play a crucial role in transitioning between related subjects smoothly. Maintaining an open posture, making eye contact, and using appropriate gestures can help convey the intention to continue the conversation and explore related topics. Similarly, a conversationalist's tone and inflection can signal a shift in subject, guiding the flow of conversation without causing disruptions. When used effectively, these non-verbal cues enhance the naturalness of transitioning between related subjects. Transitioning naturally between related subjects is an essential skill for effective conversation. By employing techniques such as bridging statements, utilizing shared experiences, and building upon previous remarks, individuals can seamlessly move from one topic to another, maintaining engagement and momentum. Non-verbal cues play a vital role in guiding the flow of conversation without causing disruptions. With practice and conscious effort, one can become a skilled conversationalist, adept at smoothly transitioning between related subjects, fostering meaningful and engaging discussions.

SEEKING INPUT FROM OTHERS TO GUIDE THE DIRECTION OF THE CONVERSATION

Another important aspect of being a good conversationalist is seeking input from others to guide the direction of the conversation. This means allowing others to have their say and actively listening to their perspectives and opinions. By doing so, one demonstrates a genuine interest in what the other person has to say and acknowledges that their input is valuable. Seeking input from others also helps in fostering a sense of inclusiveness and creating a balanced conversation. When individuals are encouraged to express their thoughts and ideas, it not only enhances the overall quality of the conversation but also promotes healthy engagement and participation from all parties involved.

Seeking input from others also helps in avoiding a one-sided conversation where only one person dominates the discussion. By actively inviting others to contribute, the conversationalist ensures that all viewpoints are considered and that the conversation is not solely centered around their own interests or opinions. This collaborative approach allows for a broader range of topics and perspectives to be discussed, resulting in a more enriching and engaging conversation for everyone involved.

Seeking input from others can help in building rapport and establishing connections with individuals. It shows that the conversationalist values the thoughts and feelings of others, and is willing to create a space where everyone's voice is heard. This can foster a sense of belonging and encourage a more open and trusting atmosphere, making individuals more likely to feel comfortable sharing their ideas and experiences. Seeking input from others can also lead to the discovery of new information and insights that one may not have been aware of before. Different individuals bring diverse knowledge and perspectives to the conversation, which can broaden one's understanding of various topics and promote personal growth and intellectual curiosity.

Seeking input from others does not imply a complete surrender of one's own stance or opinion. It is important to strike a balance between actively listening to others and expressing one's thoughts and ideas. A good conversationalist should be able to articulate their own perspective while still respecting and valuing the input provided by others. This reciprocity helps in sustaining a healthy and constructive conversation, where different viewpoints are acknowledged and understood.

Seeking input from others is a vital component of being a good conversationalist. By actively listening to others and allowing them to guide the direction of the conversation, one promotes inclusivity, encourages balanced participation, and fosters connections with individuals. Seeking input also leads to the discovery of new information and ideas, expanding one's knowledge and promoting personal growth. Balancing one's own perspective with the input of others is key in maintaining a healthy and constructive conversation. By seeking input from others, a good conversationalist can create a dynamic and engaging exchange where everyone's voice is heard and valued.

Regardless of the conversation topic, it is crucial to maintain an open and attentive mindset to become a good conversationalist. Being genuinely interested in what others have to say is an essential element that can foster a positive and engaging conversation. Active listening includes maintaining eye contact, nodding occasionally, and using verbal cues to indicate understanding and interest. By doing so, not only do you show respect and appreciation towards the person speaking, but you also encourage them to continue sharing. Being empathetic and understanding allows you to relate to the emotions and experiences that the speaker shares, which helps to build a strong connection and promote a more meaningful exchange of ideas.

Nonverbal cues play an important role in effective communication, as they aid in conveying emotions and intentions. For instance, displaying a relaxed posture and maintaining an open body position can signal approachability and receptiveness. Conversely, crossing arms or fidgeting may imply discomfort or disinterest, possibly hindering the flow of conversation. Mirroring the speaker's gestures and expressions can create a sense of rapport, making them feel more at ease and leading to a more engaging exchange. These nonverbal behaviors can significantly impact the outcome of a conversation and should be carefully considered and utilized to enhance communication.

It is essential to show respect for the speaker's opinions and avoid interrupting or imposing personal beliefs. Active participation entails asking open-ended questions that encourage the speaker to elaborate on their thoughts and feelings. By allowing them to express themselves fully, you demonstrate a genuine interest in their perspective and open the door for deeper and more meaningful exchanges. Offering validation and positive feedback can also enhance the conversational experience by boosting the speaker's confidence and encouraging them to share more. Being aware of one's own biases and avoiding judgmental attitudes can foster a more inclusive and respectful conversation. Recognizing and appreciating diversity in opinions and experiences can lead to a richer exchange of ideas and allow for personal growth and understanding. Creating a safe and nonthreatening environment is crucial for encouraging open dialogue, as people are more likely to share their thoughts and experiences when they feel valued and respected.

Becoming a good conversationalist requires active listening, empathy, and open-mindedness. Utilizing verbal and nonverbal cues, such as active listening behaviors and appropriate body language, can significantly influence the success of a conversation. Showing respect for differing opinions and actively engaging with the speaker by asking open-ended questions can enhance the quality of the exchange. Fostering a safe and inclusive environment can promote open dialogue and contribute to personal growth and understanding. By cultivating these skills and approaches, one can become a good conversationalist capable of meaningful and enriching conversations.

XII. AVOIDING COMMON PITFALLS

In order to become a good conversationalist, it is crucial to avoid common traps and pitfalls that may hinder effective communication. One such pitfall is failing to actively listen to the other person. Often, individuals focus more on formulating their responses rather than genuinely understanding what the speaker is trying to convey. By doing so, important details might be overlooked, leading to misunderstandings or misinterpretations. Another common mistake is interrupting others while they are speaking. This indicates a lack of respect and consideration for the speaker's thoughts and opinions. Interrupting may disrupt the flow of the conversation, making it difficult for both parties to engage fully. A common pitfall that many conversationalists fall into is monopolizing the conversation. Some individuals tend to dominate discussions by constantly talking about themselves or their own experiences without giving others a chance to contribute. This behavior not only creates an imbalanced dynamic but also prevents the exploration of diverse perspectives and ideas. Another challenge to overcome is the use of improper body language. Nonverbal cues such as crossed arms, constant fidgeting, or avoiding eye contact can convey disinterest or discomfort, ultimately hindering the establishment of a meaningful connection. A common mistake that can hinder effective communication is holding preconceived notions or biases about the other person or their ideas, leading to a closed-minded approach. This type of mindset can prevent individuals from truly engaging with the conversation and learning from different viewpoints. It is essential to avoid distractions such as checking one's phone or allowing external factors to take the focus away from the conversation. This can be perceived as rude and disrespectful, providing a clear indication that the speaker's words do not hold importance. To avoid these pitfalls, it is important to cultivate active listening skills. By fully engaging with the speaker's words and providing nonverbal cues that indicate genuine interest, one can foster a climate of open and meaningful communication. Allowing others to finish speaking before offering one's own thoughts and opinions demonstrates respect and consideration for their input. Practicing self-awareness and actively monitoring one's contributions can help prevent monopolizing conversations and promote a balanced exchange of ideas. It is also crucial to be mindful of body language, ensuring that it conveys attentiveness and openness. By maintaining an open mind and being willing to challenge preconceived notions, individuals can foster a more inclusive and enriching conversation. Eliminating distractions and giving one's full attention to the speaker is key to creating an environment where personal connections can be formed and ideas can be shared freely.

Becoming a good conversationalist requires awareness of common pitfalls and a conscious effort to avoid them. By actively listening, refraining from interruptions, sharing the conversation, displaying appropriate body language, keeping an open mind, and minimizing distractions, individuals can enhance their communication skills and establish meaningful connections with others. These strategies contribute to fostering an environment where ideas can be exchanged, personal growth can be fostered, and relationships can be strengthened.

JUDGING, CRITICIZING, OR INTERRUPTING OTHERS

When engaging in conversation, it is crucial to adopt a non-judgmental and open-minded attitude. Judging or criticizing others' viewpoints can not only hurt their feelings but also hinder the flow of the discussion. Rather than immediately passing judgment, it is important to listen attentively and consider the merits of what others are saying. Each person brings a unique perspective to the conversation, and by dismissing or criticizing their ideas, we miss out on the opportunity to learn from one another. Interrupting others when they are speaking can be seen as disrespectful and disruptive, as it prevents them from fully expressing their thoughts and ideas. Interrupting can convey a sense of impatience or superiority, neither of which contributes to a healthy and productive conversation. Instead, it is crucial to patiently wait for an appropriate moment to interject or ask questions, allowing for a respectful exchange of ideas and ensuring that everyone has a chance to be heard. Interrupting others may inadvertently shut down valuable contributions, potentially limiting the breadth and depth of the conversation. By actively listening and valuing others' input, we can foster a more inclusive and enriching conversation.

To become a skilled conversationalist, it is essential to cultivate self-awareness and Mindfulness. Becoming aware of our tendency to judge, criticize, or interrupt others allows us to make a conscious effort to change our behavior. It requires a shift in mindset, adopting an attitude of curiosity and empathy. This can be achieved by practicing active listening, which involves not only hearing but truly understanding what others are saying. When we actively listen, we are fully present in the conversation, giving our undivided attention and seeking to comprehend the speaker's point of view. This allows for a deeper connection between participants and encourages a more meaningful exchange of ideas. Practicing empathy can aid in refraining from making snap judgments or criticisms. Empathy involves putting ourselves in others' shoes, attempting to understand their perspective and emotions. By considering the reasons behind someone's viewpoint and their personal experiences, we can approach conversations with a greater degree of empathy and compassion. This not only promotes more harmonious interactions but also broadens our own horizons and fosters personal growth.

Judging, criticizing, or interrupting others undermines the essence of good conversational skills. By adopting a non-judgmental and open-minded approach, actively listening, and practicing empathy, we can create a positive and enriching atmosphere for fruitful discussions. It is through understanding and valuing diverse viewpoints that we can truly expand our knowledge and foster genuine connections with others. So let us strive to be better conversationalists by setting aside our judgments, treating others with respect, and embracing the gift of dialogue.

CULTIVATING AWARENESS OF ONE'S OWN BIASES

Cultivating awareness of one's own biases is essential for becoming a good conversationalist. Biases are inherent in every individual and are shaped by various factors such as upbringing, cultural background, and personal experiences. These biases can greatly influence the way we perceive and interpret information, leading to a distorted view of the world. By acknowledging and understanding our own biases, we can better navigate conversations and engage in open-minded and respectful dialogue. This process requires self-reflection and a willingness to challenge our preconceived notions. Firstly, becoming aware of our biases allows us to recognize the limitations of our own knowledge. It is natural to form opinions based on our experiences and beliefs, but it is important to recognize that these opinions may not always align with objective reality. By acknowledging our biases, we can approach conversations with a sense of humility, recognizing that there is always more to learn and understand. This awareness allows us to be more receptive to new ideas and alternative perspectives, fostering a more productive exchange of information. Being conscious of our biases enables us to engage in more empathetic conversations. Biases tend to create barriers between individuals with differing viewpoints, as we often gravitate towards confirming our existing beliefs rather than seeking understanding. When we are aware of our biases, we can actively challenge them and strive to understand the perspectives of others with an open mind. This cultivates a sense of empathy and allows us to connect with others on a deeper level, even if we may disagree.

Understanding our biases promotes self-growth and personal development. By critically examining our own beliefs and prejudices, we can address any irrational or unfair judgments we may hold. This self-reflection allows us to evolve as individuals and expand our worldview. Engaging in conversations with a genuine desire to understand others, rather than just asserting our own opinions, can lead to personal growth and intellectual enrichment. Cultivating awareness of biases fosters a more inclusive society. It is no secret that biases can reinforce social inequalities and perpetuate stereotypes. By actively understanding and challenging these biases, we can contribute to a more inclusive and accepting community. By approaching conversations with a willingness to learn and understand different perspectives, we can break down barriers and create an environment where all voices are heard and respected. Cultivating awareness of one's own biases is crucial to becoming a good conversationalist. Recognizing the limitations of our own knowledge, engaging in empathetic conversations, promoting personal development, and contributing to an inclusive society are all outcomes of understanding and challenging our biases. It requires self-reflection, openness, and a willingness to question our own beliefs. By doing so, we can foster more meaningful and enriching conversations that have the potential to build bridges, break down barriers, and ultimately lead to personal growth and mutual understanding.

PRACTICING PATIENCE AND ACTIVE LISTENING

Practicing patience and active listening are two crucial skills that contribute to becoming a good conversationalist. Patience is essential in any conversation as it allows individuals to take a step back and calmly listen to what the other person is saying. Without patience, there is a risk of interrupting or dominating the conversation, which can hinder effective communication. Beyond just waiting for one's turn to speak, being patient also involves being open-minded and non-judgmental towards the speaker's perspective. By patiently listening, individuals can gain insights into others' opinions, experiences, and emotions, leading to a more profound understanding and connection.

Active listening goes hand in hand with patience as it involves fully engaging with the speaker and demonstrating genuine interest in their words. This form of listening is not merely passive but requires concentration, focus, and empathy. Active listeners make a conscious effort to understand the speaker's ideas, feelings, and intentions, which helps create an atmosphere of trust and respect. They engage in non-verbal cues, such as nodding or maintaining eye contact, to show their attentiveness. Active listeners ask thoughtful questions and provide feedback that encourages the speaker to delve deeper into their thoughts and feelings. This type of listening fosters a sense of validation and allows for a more meaningful exchange of ideas.

Both patience and active listening can also aid in overcoming potential barriers to effective communication. Impatience often leads to interrupting or finishing someone's sentences, which can be perceived as disrespectful or dismissive. By practicing patience, individuals give others the necessary space and time to express themselves fully, enabling the conversation to flow more smoothly. Active listening, on the other hand, helps individuals avoid misunderstandings or misinterpretations that may arise from selective listening or preconceived assumptions. By engaging in active listening, individuals build a bridge of understanding and create an environment where both parties feel heard and valued. Practicing patience and active listening contributes to the development of strong interpersonal skills. These skills are not only essential in social interactions but also crucial in professional contexts. Employers value individuals who are patient and attentive listeners, as they tend to be excellent team players and problem solvers. These skills can positively impact personal relationships by fostering empathy, reducing conflicts, and building stronger connections. Patience and active listening are fundamental skills that contribute to becoming a good conversationalist. By practicing patience, individuals can create a space for meaningful communication and gain a deeper understanding of others. Active listening, with its focus on attentiveness, empathy, and engagement, leads to effective and fulfilling conversations. These skills help overcome barriers to communication and contribute to the development of strong interpersonal relationships. Whether in personal or professional settings, patience and active listening are invaluable tools that enable individuals to connect with others and enhance their overall communication capabilities.

FOCUSING ON ONESELF INSTEAD OF THE SPEAKER

This is a common pitfall in conversations. It is an unfortunate tendency of human nature to prioritize our own thoughts, opinions, and experiences over those of others. When this occurs, we become more concerned with formulating our response and making sure our voice is heard, rather than genuinely listening to what the speaker has to say. This self-centered focus can be detrimental to the quality of the conversation and hinder the development of meaningful connections. Conversations should be a two-way street, allowing both parties to express their thoughts and feelings. When we are solely focused on our own needs, we miss out on the opportunity to truly understand and empathize with the speaker. This can lead to misunderstandings, miscommunication, and a lack of respect for the speaker's viewpoint. Constantly redirecting the conversation back to ourselves can make the other person feel marginalized, unimportant, and unheard. This can create a negative dynamic where the speaker may feel discouraged from sharing their thoughts and may opt to disengage from the conversation altogether. It is important to remember that conversations are not just about expressing ourselves but also about learning from others and broadening our perspectives. By shifting our focus from ourselves to the speaker, we can actively show interest and engage in active listening. Active listening involves not only hearing the words that are spoken but also paying attention to non-verbal cues, such as body language and facial expressions, which can convey emotions and deeper meaning. Engaging in active listening demonstrates respect, empathy, and a genuine interest in the speaker's thoughts and experiences. It requires setting aside our own ego and being fully present in the moment. By doing so, we allow the conversation to flow naturally and foster a sense of collaboration and mutual understanding. To refocus our attention on the speaker, we can employ techniques such as paraphrasing and asking open-ended questions. Paraphrasing involves restating the speaker's ideas in our own words to ensure that we have understood them correctly. This not only confirms our engagement but also allows the speaker to clarify any misunderstandings. Open-ended questions, on the other hand, encourage the speaker to elaborate and provide more information, thus keeping the conversation flowing and deepening our understanding. By consciously avoiding the pitfall of focusing on oneself and instead placing importance on the speaker, we can become better conversationalists and develop stronger connections with others.

SHOWING GENUINE INTEREST IN OTHERS' PERSPECTIVES

To engage in meaningful and fruitful conversations, it is imperative to move beyond a self-centered approach and actively listen to others. This means being genuinely curious about their thoughts, opinions, and experiences, and demonstrating empathy towards their perspectives. Genuine interest in others' perspectives allows for a deeper understanding of diverse viewpoints and fosters an environment of mutual respect and openness. One way to demonstrate genuine interest in others' perspectives is by practicing active listening. Active listening involves giving undivided attention to the speaker and actively responding to their comments and questions. By doing so, one can show that they are truly invested in what the person is saying and are willing to attentively engage in the conversation. This not only encourages the speaker to share more but also indicates that their perspective is valued and respected.

Another crucial aspect of showing genuine interest in others' perspectives is the ability to suspend personal judgments and biases. It is natural for individuals to have their own preconceived notions and beliefs, but allowing these biases to overshadow the conversation can hinder true understanding and empathy. By stepping back and temporarily setting aside personal biases, a good conversationalist can create a safe and open space for the speaker to freely express their ideas and opinions. In addition, a good conversationalist understands the importance of asking meaningful and open-ended questions. These types of questions invite others to elaborate on their perspectives, allowing for a more in-depth exploration of their thoughts and experiences. By asking questions such as "How do you feel about this issue?" or "Can you provide an example to illustrate your point?", the conversationalist encourages the speaker to delve deeper into their perspective and facilitates a richer conversation. Showing genuine interest in others' perspectives involves acknowledging and validating their emotions. As humans, emotions play a significant role in shaping our perspectives and experiences. A good conversationalist recognizes this and responds empathetically, reflecting an understanding of the speaker's emotions. By acknowledging and validating their emotions, the conversationalist empathizes with the speaker's perspective and establishes a deeper connection.

A good conversationalist seeks to learn from others and expand their own knowledge and understanding. By being open-minded and receptive to different perspectives, one can broaden their horizons and gain new insights. Cultivating a genuine interest in others' perspectives allows for personal growth and development. Showing genuine interest in others' perspectives is an integral aspect of being a good conversationalist. By actively listening, suspending personal judgments, asking meaningful questions, acknowledging and validating emotions, and seeking to learn from others, a good conversationalist can create inclusive and enriching conversations. This not only strengthens interpersonal connections but also facilitates the exchange of diverse ideas and promotes a more inclusive and understanding society.

RESISTING THE URGE TO CONSTANTLY REDIRECT THE CONVERSATION TO PERSONAL EXPERIENCES

One key aspect of being a good conversationalist is resisting the urge to constantly redirect the conversation to personal experiences. While sharing personal stories can enhance the conversation and make it more engaging, it is important not to dominate the discussion solely with one's own experiences. Instead, a good conversationalist understands the need for balance and actively listens to others' perspectives, experiences, and opinions. By doing so, the conversationalist shows respect for the other person's ideas, fosters a sense of inclusion, and creates space for diverse viewpoints to be heard.

Redirecting conversations to personal experiences can often stem from a deep-rooted desire to connect and relate to others. Constantly redirecting the conversation in this manner can unintentionally shift the focus away from the other person's thoughts and feelings, making them feel unheard or undervalued. Repetitive storytelling can be tiring for the listener, as it inhibits the opportunity for them to contribute their own unique input to the conversation. Being mindful of these tendencies can lead to more meaningful and balanced interactions. Rather than instinctively interjecting with personal experiences, a good conversationalist actively listens and asks thoughtful questions to encourage the other person to share their own stories. By actively engaging in the conversation in this way, the conversationalist shows genuine interest in the other person's perspectives, creating an atmosphere of mutual respect and understanding. Resisting the urge to constantly redirect the conversation to personal experiences allows for the exploration of different topics and ideas. By allowing the dialogue to naturally unfold, individuals can tap into a wider range of knowledge and experiences beyond their own. This not only enriches the conversation but also promotes personal growth and intellectual curiosity. Being conscious of the conversation's trajectory ensures that everyone has the opportunity to contribute and be heard. Dominating the discussion with personal experiences can inadvertently silence others, hindering the potential for constructive dialogue and the exchange of ideas. Recognizing and respecting the diversity of perspectives in a conversation cultivates an environment that is inclusive, respectful, and collaborative. Being a good conversationalist requires resisting the urge to constantly redirect the conversation to personal experiences. By actively listening, asking thoughtful questions, and valuing other people's perspectives, a good conversationalist creates a balanced and inclusive dialogue. This approach not only enhances the depth and quality of the conversation but also fosters mutual respect and understanding. By consciously avoiding the temptation to dominate the discussion with personal stories, a good conversationalist ensures that everyone has the opportunity to contribute, ultimately enriching the conversation and fostering a positive and engaging atmosphere.

To be a good conversationalist, it is crucial to develop active listening skills. Active listening involves fully engaging with the speaker, both verbally and non-verbally. One way to demonstrate active listening is through the use of appropriate body language, such as maintaining eye contact and nodding along to indicate understanding and interest in what the speaker is saying. By doing so, the listener creates an environment of trust and respect, which encourages the speaker to share their thoughts and feelings openly. Paraphrasing and summarizing the speaker's point can further demonstrate active listening and understanding of the conversation. This not only shows that the listener is paying attention, but also helps to clarify any misunderstandings and ensures that both individuals are on the same page. Another important aspect of being a good conversationalist is asking open-ended questions. Open-ended questions allow for a more in-depth and meaningful conversation, as they prompt the speaker to provide detailed and thoughtful responses. These types of questions often begin with words like "how", "why", or "what", and encourage the speaker to share their opinions, experiences, or feelings. By asking open-ended questions, the listener demonstrates a genuine interest in the conversation and the speaker's perspective, which helps to build rapport and establish a connection. Being aware of one's own body language and verbal cues is essential in becoming a good conversationalist. Non-verbal cues, such as facial expressions, hand gestures, and tone of voice, can greatly impact the overall communication experience. Projecting a friendly and approachable demeanor can help put the speaker at ease and create a comfortable atmosphere for discussion. Similarly, maintaining a positive and supportive tone while speaking can help foster a constructive and engaging conversation. In addition to active listening and effective questioning, it is crucial to cultivate empathy and understanding during conversations. Empathy involves the ability to put oneself in the speaker's shoes and genuinely understand their emotions and perspectives. By demonstrating empathy, the listener not only validates the speaker's feelings but also creates an environment where they feel heard and understood. This, in turn, encourages further engagement and promotes a more meaningful and impactful conversation.

Becoming a good conversationalist requires the development of various skills. Active listening, through the use of appropriate body language and paraphrasing, is essential for demonstrating engagement and understanding. Asking open-ended questions encourages detailed and thoughtful responses, facilitating a deeper conversation. Being aware of one's own body language and verbal cues helps create a comfortable and welcoming environment. Cultivating empathy and understanding allows for a more meaningful and impactful conversation. By consistently practicing these skills, one can become a skilled conversationalist capable of fostering genuine connections and meaningful dialogues.

XIII. PRACTICING MINDFULNESS IN CONVERSATIONS

Mindfulness, a concept deeply rooted in Buddhist philosophy, is gaining increasing recognition and prominence in a range of fields, including psychology and communication. When applied to conversations, Mindfulness plays a pivotal role in fostering effective and meaningful exchanges. In essence, Mindfulness in conversations refers to the practice of being fully present and engaged in the dialogue, encompassing both listening and speaking. By employing Mindfulness, individuals can not only improve their ability to comprehend the message being conveyed, but also enhance their own self-awareness and empathy towards others. Engaging in mindful conversations necessitates the cultivation of active listening skills. Many individuals tend to listen with the intent to respond rather than to understand. Mindfulness, Encourages individuals to adopt a different approach – one that emphasizes truly hearing and comprehending the words being spoken. This practice requires individuals to suspend judgment and detach themselves from their own internal dialogue, allowing them to fully absorb the speaker's words and intentions. By being fully present and attentive, individuals can avoid the pitfalls of misunderstanding or misinterpretation, thus fostering a deeper sense of connection and empathy.

Mindfulness in conversations extends beyond listening, encompassing the notion of self-awareness. Mindful speakers are cognizant of their own thoughts, emotions, and body language, which enables them to express themselves in a clear and authentic way. By actively monitoring their own internal state, individuals can communicate with honesty and integrity, ensuring that their message accurately reflects their intentions. The ability to regulate one's emotions is particularly crucial in difficult conversations, as individuals practicing Mindfulness can navigate challenging interactions with equanimity and grace.

Another crucial aspect of practicing Mindfulness in conversations is the cultivation of empathy. Empathy serves as the foundation for meaningful connections and true understanding among individuals. Through Mindfulness, individuals can develop a profound sense of empathy, by fully immersing themselves in the experiences and perspectives of others. By suspending their own judgments and preconceived notions, mindful conversationalists can create a safe space for the speaker to express themselves freely, without the fear of being misunderstood or invalidated. Through this empathetic exchange, individuals can gradually develop a sense of shared understanding and connection, fostering harmonious relationships. Mindfulness in conversations serves as a fundamental tool for becoming a good conversationalist. By embodying the principles of active listening, self-awareness, and empathy, individuals can transform their communication skills, ultimately leading to more authentic and fulfilling interactions. Through the practice of Mindfulness, conversations can transcend mere exchanges of words, becoming transformative experiences that cultivate deeper connections and mutual understanding. By embracing Mindfulness in conversations, individuals can unlock the true potential of effective communication, ultimately fostering an atmosphere of empathy and connection.

BEING FULLY PRESENT IN THE MOMENT

Being fully present in the moment is a crucial aspect of being a good conversationalist. When engaging in a conversation, it is essential to give undivided attention to the other person. This means putting away any distractions, such as cellphones or other electronic devices, and focusing solely on the conversation at hand. By doing so, one shows respect for the speaker and indicates genuine interest in what they have to say. Being fully present in the moment allows for a deeper level of connection and understanding between individuals. When one is fully engaged in a conversation, they are able to pick up on subtleties in the speaker's tone of voice, body language, and facial expressions, which can provide valuable insights into their thoughts and feelings. Being present in the moment allows for active listening, which is a fundamental skill for effective communication. Active listening entails not only hearing the words being spoken but also paying attention to the speaker's emotions, intentions, and context. By actively listening, one can respond to the speaker's needs and contribute to a meaningful conversation. Being fully present in the moment during a conversation fosters a sense of Mindfulness. Mindfulness involves being aware of one's thoughts, emotions, and sensations without judgment. When one is present in the moment, they are attuned to their own experiences as well as the experiences of others, which can lead to a deeper understanding of oneself and one's connection to the world around them. Being present in the moment allows for more meaningful and authentic interactions. When one is fully engaged in a conversation, they are more likely to express their true thoughts and feelings, as well as listen to others with an open mind. This creates an atmosphere of trust and vulnerability, fostering deeper connections and more fulfilling conversations. On the other hand, not being fully present in the moment hinders effective communication. When one is distracted or preoccupied during a conversation, they may miss important details or fail to recognize the needs and emotions of the speaker. This can lead to misunderstandings, misinterpretations, and a breakdown in communication. Not being present in the moment during a conversation can convey disinterest or lack of respect, which can be detrimental to the relationship between individuals. Being fully present in the moment is vital for being a good conversationalist. It enables active listening, promotes Mindfulness, and facilitates more meaningful interactions. Conversely, not being present in the moment can hinder effective communication and result in miscommunications or strained relationships. To be a good conversationalist, one must cultivate the ability to be fully present in the moment during conversations.

MINIMIZING DISTRACTIONS AND MULTITASKING

One important aspect of being a good conversationalist is minimizing distractions and avoiding multitasking. In today's digital age, it is easy to get distracted by our phones, laptops, and other gadgets. When engaging in a conversation, it is crucial to give our undivided attention to the person we are talking to. This means putting away our devices, turning off notifications, and focusing on the present moment. By doing so, we signal to the other person that we value their presence and what they have to say. Multitasking can severely hinder our ability to actively listen and engage in meaningful conversations. When we try to do several things at once, our attention becomes divided, and we are unable to fully comprehend and respond to the conversation. Multitasking can lead to misunderstandings and misinterpretations, as our focus is not solely on the interaction at hand. It is essential to prioritize our conversations and give them our full attention. By minimizing distractions and avoiding multitasking, we create a conducive environment for effective communication and enhance our conversational skills.

GIVING UNDIVIDED ATTENTION TO THE SPEAKER

When engaged in a conversation, it is essential to focus one's attention solely on the speaker, as it allows for deeper understanding and meaningful connections. By giving undivided attention, the listener shows respect and interest in what the speaker has to say, creating a comfortable environment for open communication. One way to demonstrate undivided attention is through non-verbal cues, such as maintaining eye contact with the speaker. Eye contact not only shows that one is actively listening but also conveys a sense of genuineness and empathy. It empowers the speaker, making them feel heard and valued. Another way to exhibit undivided attention is through attentive body language. This entails facing the speaker directly, leaning in slightly to show interest, and nodding along to indicate understanding. These non-verbal cues serve as positive reinforcement, encouraging the speaker to continue expressing their thoughts and feelings honestly. Giving undivided attention requires mental presence. It is important to refrain from distractions such as checking one's phone or allowing the mind to wander. This signifies that the speaker's words are prioritized and respected. Active listening is an integral part of giving undivided attention. It involves making a conscious effort to fully understand and absorb the speaker's message. This can be achieved by paraphrasing and summarizing what the speaker has said, allowing for clarification and confirmation of comprehension. Asking open-ended questions demonstrates engagement and encourages the speaker to delve deeper into their thoughts and experiences. By actively listening, the listener displays empathy and appreciation for the speaker's perspective, fostering a stronger connection and trust. Giving undivided attention entails withholding judgment and offering support. It is crucial to create a judgment-free space where the speaker feels safe to share their thoughts and emotions openly. Being mindful of one's own biases and remaining open-minded fosters a sense of understanding and collaboration. Offering support through affirmations and genuine praise uplifts the speaker, boosting their confidence and encouraging further conversation. Giving undivided attention to the speaker is fundamental to being a good conversationalist. It involves utilizing non-verbal cues, such as eye contact and attentive body language, to show respect, interest, and empathy. Mental presence and active listening are essential in fully understanding and engaging with the speaker's message. Withholding judgment and offering support create a safe and open space for honest communication. By implementing these strategies, one can foster meaningful connections and enhance the quality of conversations, ultimately becoming a proficient conversationalist.

APPRECIATING THE VALUE OF EACH CONVERSATION

In today's fast-paced world, where interactions often occur through digital means, we sometimes forget the importance of meaningful conversations. Each conversation presents an opportunity for personal growth and enlightenment. By appreciating the value of each interaction, we establish a foundation for cultivating deep connections and understanding between individuals. Recognizing the worth of every conversation can help foster empathy and promote active listening skills, two crucial components of effective communication. By truly valuing each conversation, we demonstrate respect for the thoughts, ideas, and experiences shared by others. It is through these exchanges that we expand our horizons, challenge our preconceived notions, and gain new perspectives on the world around us.

One way to appreciate the value of each conversation is by being fully present and engaged during interactions. In our digital age, it is easy to become distracted or detached, scrolling through our smartphones or thinking ahead to the next task on our to-do list. To truly appreciate the value of each conversation, we must give our undivided attention to the person speaking. This means actively listening, maintaining eye contact, and responding thoughtfully. By doing so, we not only demonstrate our interest and respect for the other person, but we also create an environment conducive to open and honest dialogue.

It is important to recognize that every conversation holds the potential for personal growth and learning. Even seemingly mundane or casual discussions can offer opportunities for self-reflection and insight. By approaching each conversation with an open mind and a willingness to learn, we embrace the value of diverse perspectives and ideas. By actively seeking out differing opinions, we can broaden our own understanding of the world and challenge our own biases.

Appreciating the value of each conversation means recognizing that every person has a unique story to tell. Each individual we encounter possesses a wealth of knowledge and experiences that we can learn from. By approaching conversations with curiosity and a genuine desire to understand others, we foster an environment of inclusivity and respect. This not only enriches our own understanding of the world but also demonstrates empathy and compassion towards others. In doing so, we cultivate meaningful connections and establish a sense of community.

Appreciating the value of each conversation is fundamental to becoming a good conversationalist. By being fully present and engaged, seeking personal growth and learning from every interaction, and recognizing the unique perspectives and experiences of others, we establish a strong foundation for effective communication. By embracing the worth of each conversation, we not only enrich our own lives but also contribute to the development of a more empathetic and interconnected society. To be a good conversationalist is to recognize and appreciate the transformative power of conversation in fostering understanding, growth, and connection.

SEEING CONVERSATIONS AS OPPORTUNITIES FOR GROWTH AND CONNECTION

In order to become a good conversationalist, it is crucial to see conversations as opportunities for growth and connection. When we approach conversations with an open mind and a willingness to learn from others, we not only expand our knowledge but also establish meaningful connections with those we interact with. By viewing conversations as opportunities for growth, we can actively engage in the exchange of ideas, perspectives, and experiences. This mindset allows us to broaden our horizons and gain insights that we may not have considered before. For example, when engaging in a conversation with someone who holds different beliefs or values, we can choose to listen with the intention of understanding their perspective rather than simply debating or dismissing their opinions. This not only fosters empathy but also encourages personal development by challenging our own preconceived notions and expanding our understanding of the world. Seeing conversations as opportunities for connection enables us to build genuine relationships with others. When we approach conversations with the goal of establishing a connection, we can engage in active listening and show genuine interest in the other person. This involves not only paying attention to their words but also being attuned to their non-verbal cues and emotions. By doing so, we demonstrate our respect for their individuality and create an environment of trust and mutual understanding. Through these meaningful connections, we not only enhance our social interactions but also have the chance to learn from the experiences and wisdom of others.

Viewing conversations as opportunities for growth and connection allows us to foster personal and professional development. By actively seeking out conversations with individuals who possess diverse perspectives and experiences, we expose ourselves to new ideas and insights. This exposure not only expands our knowledge but also challenges us to think critically and consider alternative viewpoints. Engaging in conversations with professionals in our desired field can provide valuable mentorship and guidance. By actively seeking out these opportunities for growth, we can refine our communication skills, gain new perspectives, and broaden our professional networks. Perceiving conversations as opportunities for growth and connection is essential for becoming a good conversationalist. By embracing conversations as chances to expand our knowledge, establish meaningful connections, and foster personal and professional development, we can enhance our communication skills and create a more inclusive and engaging environment. It is through this mindset that we can truly appreciate the value of conversations and the potential they hold for our personal and collective growth.

ACKNOWLEDGING THE UNIQUE PERSPECTIVES AND EXPERIENCES SHARED BY OTHERS

In the pursuit of becoming a good conversationalist, it is essential to acknowledge and appreciate the unique perspectives and experiences shared by others. Every individual brings a distinct background and set of life experiences, which shape their beliefs, values, and opinions. By recognizing and valuing these differences, we open up the possibility for meaningful and enriching conversations. One way to achieve this is by practicing active listening. Rather than simply waiting for our turn to speak, active listening involves genuinely focusing on the speaker, comprehending their message, and responding appropriately. This approach allows us to fully immerse ourselves in their words, demonstrating our respect and attentiveness. Acknowledging the uniqueness of others requires us to suspend judgment and avoid making assumptions. It is easy to fall into the trap of assuming that our own perspectives are superior or more valid than others', but this only serves to hinder genuine dialogue. Instead, we should strive to approach conversations with an open mind and a willingness to consider alternative viewpoints. This can be achieved by asking open-ended questions and actively seeking to understand the reasoning behind someone's beliefs or opinions. Embracing curiosity and a genuine desire to learn from others fosters an inclusive environment where diverse voices are heard and valued. Acknowledging the unique perspectives and experiences shared by others also involves recognizing and celebrating the diversity of cultures and backgrounds. Our world is composed of a rich tapestry of cultural, ethnic, and social differences, each offering a distinctive viewpoint on various topics. When engaging in conversations, it is crucial to acknowledge the influence of cultural context and inherent biases that shape individuals' perspectives. By actively seeking to understand and appreciate these differences, we create a conducive atmosphere for meaningful and respectful exchanges. Engaging in cross-cultural conversations and learning about various traditions and practices not only broadens our own understanding but also fosters empathy and respect for diverse perspectives. This inclusive approach to conversations encourages equal participation and provides an opportunity for all voices to be heard, eliminating marginalization and exclusion.

Becoming a good conversationalist requires a keen awareness and appreciation of the unique perspectives and experiences shared by others. Practicing active listening, suspending judgment, and embracing cultural diversity are all essential components of acknowledging and valuing the diversity of human experiences. By engaging in meaningful conversations that respect different viewpoints, we create a space where everyone feels heard, respected, and understood. This open-minded and inclusive approach to conversations not only fosters personal growth but also enhances our ability to connect with others in a deeply meaningful way. Only by acknowledging and valuing the richness of human experiences can we truly become effective conversationalists and agents of positive change in our interconnected world. Being a good conversationalist is a valuable skill to possess, as it allows individuals to connect with others on a deeper level and build meaningful relationships. To be successful in conversation, there are several key qualities and strategies that one should employ. Firstly, active listening is essential. This means fully engaging in the conversation, paying attention to both verbal and nonverbal cues, and showing genuine interest in what the other person is saying. By actively listening, one not only demonstrates respect and empathy, but also gains a deeper understanding of the topic at hand. Asking open-ended questions is crucial in fostering meaningful dialogue. Open-ended questions encourage the other person to share their thoughts and feelings, rather than just providing simple, one-word answers. This creates a more dynamic conversation and allows both parties to learn and grow from the exchange of ideas. A good conversationalist should strive to be well-informed and knowledgeable about a wide range of subjects. This not only helps to keep the conversation flowing, but also allows for the exploration of new and interesting topics. Staying informed can be achieved through reading, listening to podcasts, or engaging in meaningful discussions with others. Being mindful of nonverbal communication is essential. This includes maintaining eye contact, using appropriate facial expressions and gestures, and being mindful of body language. Nonverbal cues often provide additional insights into what the other person is thinking or feeling, and being aware of these cues can help improve the overall understanding and flow of the conversation. Being mindful of one's own speech patterns and mannerisms is important in being a good conversationalist. Avoiding excessive interruptions, using appropriate pauses and inflections, and speaking clearly and concisely all contribute to effective communication. A good conversationalist should also strive to create an inclusive and welcoming environment. This can be achieved by allowing everyone in the conversation an equal opportunity to speak, being respectful of others' opinions even if they differ from one's own, and avoiding judgment or criticism. By creating a safe and inclusive space, individuals are more likely to feel comfortable and open up, leading to more meaningful and engaging conversations. It is important to practice self-awareness and reflect on one's own conversational skills. Taking the time to evaluate how one communicates and actively seeking feedback from others can aid in personal growth and improvement. Recognizing and addressing any personal biases or prejudices that may affect communication is crucial in being an effective conversationalist. Being a good conversationalist requires a combination of active listening, asking open-ended questions, being knowledgeable about a variety of subjects, being mindful of nonverbal communication, and creating an inclusive environment. By employing these strategies, individuals can enhance their communication skills and build stronger connections with others.

XIV. RECOGNIZING AND RESPECTING CULTURAL DIFFERENCES

In today's increasingly globalized world, it is crucial for individuals to recognize and respect cultural differences in order to become good conversationalists. Cultural differences refer to the variations in norms, values, beliefs, and behaviors that exist among different groups of people. These differences can be influenced by factors such as nationality, ethnicity, religion, language, and even regional diversities within a country. By acknowledging and appreciating these distinctions, individuals can foster a more inclusive and harmonious environment for communication. One fundamental aspect of recognizing cultural differences is being aware that there is no universally correct way of thinking, behaving, or communicating. What may seem normal and acceptable in one culture could be considered rude or offensive in another. For instance, while direct and assertive communication is valued in some Western cultures, it may be seen as aggressive or impolite in certain Eastern cultures that prioritize indirectness and harmony. When engaging in conversation with individuals from diverse cultural backgrounds, it is essential to adapt and adjust one's communication style to ensure mutual understanding and respect. Recognizing cultural differences involves being open-minded and curious. Rather than judging or criticizing practices or beliefs that seem unfamiliar or strange, individuals should strive to approach these differences with genuine interest and a willingness to learn. By demonstrating curiosity, individuals can not only gain valuable insights into other cultures but can also develop empathy and broaden their perspectives. This willingness to learn can be exhibited through asking thoughtful questions, actively listening to others, and engaging in meaningful dialogue that encourages the sharing of perspectives and experiences. Respect for cultural differences entails avoiding stereotypes and generalizations. While certain cultural traits or behaviors may be commonly observed in a particular group, it is important to remember that not all individuals within that culture conform to these stereotypes. Assuming that everyone from a specific culture thinks or behaves in a certain way can perpetuate biases and hinder genuine understanding. Instead, individuals should approach each conversation with an open mind, suspending judgment and recognizing that each person is shaped by a complex web of cultural, personal, and individual factors. Recognizing and respecting cultural differences involves cultivating self-awareness. It is important to acknowledge and reflect upon one's own cultural background, biases, and assumptions. By understanding the influence of one's own culture on beliefs, values, and communication styles, individuals can develop a heightened sensitivity towards the perspectives and experiences of others. This self-awareness allows individuals to navigate conversations in a more respectful and inclusive manner, while also being mindful of potential misunderstandings or misinterpretations. Recognizing and respecting cultural differences is a fundamental aspect of becoming a good conversationalist. By acknowledging the variations in norms, values, beliefs, and behaviors among different cultural groups, individuals can foster inclusive and meaningful conversations. This recognition involves being open-minded, avoiding stereotypes, asking thoughtful questions, and cultivating self-awareness. By practicing these principles, individuals can bridge cultural divides, foster understanding, and create a more harmonious global community.

ADAPTING COMMUNICATION STYLES TO CULTURAL NORMS

In today's globalized world, it is not uncommon to encounter people from different cultural backgrounds. Each culture has its own set of communication norms, which may vary greatly from one another. For instance, in some cultures, maintaining direct eye contact is considered a sign of respect and attentiveness, while in others, it may be seen as confrontational or disrespectful. Similarly, the use of gestures and body language can have different meanings across cultures. For instance, a thumbs-up gesture is a positive sign in many Western countries, but it is considered offensive in certain Middle Eastern and Asian cultures. Understanding and adapting one's communication style to align with the cultural norms of the person or group being conversed with is crucial to ensure effective and respectful communication. One aspect of cultural communication norms is the use of language and idiomatic expressions. Language is the most fundamental tool of communication, and different cultures often have unique phrases and idioms that have specific meanings. Being aware of these cultural expressions can help create a sense of connection and understanding between individuals from different backgrounds. For example, in English, the phrase "break a leg" means "good luck" in the context of performing arts, but if used in a literal sense, it can be confusing or even offensive to someone unfamiliar with the idiom. It is therefore important to be mindful of linguistic differences and choose words and expressions that are easily understood and culturally appropriate. Another important consideration when adapting communication styles to cultural norms is the concept of personal space. In some cultures, such as those in Latin America, the Middle East, or Southern Europe, people tend to stand closer to each other during conversations compared to cultures like Northern Europe or North America, where personal space is highly valued. Invading someone's personal space in a conversation may make them uncomfortable or even cause misunderstandings. By observing the personal space boundaries of individuals from different cultural backgrounds, one can show respect for their norms and create a more comfortable environment for communication. Adapting communication styles to cultural norms is crucial for being a good conversationalist. Cultural differences in eye contact, gestures, language, and personal space can greatly influence the effectiveness and understanding of communication. By observing and respecting these cultural norms, individuals can foster an inclusive and respectful environment for communication, bridging the gaps between different cultures and building meaningful connections. Being mindful of cultural communication norms not only enhances one's conversational skills but also promotes intercultural understanding and appreciation.

UNDERSTANDING AND RESPECTING CULTURAL ETIQUETTE

Understanding and respecting cultural etiquette is essential in becoming a good conversationalist. In today's globalized world, where people from different cultures intermingle and interact, it is crucial to be aware of and sensitive to the varied cultural norms and customs. Every culture has its own unique set of etiquettes, which govern how individuals behave and communicate with each other. By familiarizing ourselves with these etiquettes, we can navigate social interactions with grace and avoid any unintentional offense. For instance, in Japanese culture, it is customary to bow when greeting someone as a sign of respect. Understanding this cultural norm and reciprocating the gesture shows our appreciation for their traditions. Similarly, in some Middle Eastern countries, it is considered impolite to show the soles of your feet, as they are seen as unclean. By keeping our feet flat on the ground or crossing our legs at the ankles, we demonstrate respect for their cultural customs.

Cultural etiquette is not limited to physical gestures but also extends to verbal communication. Different cultures have varying degrees of directness or indirectness in their communication styles. While Western cultures value directness and assertiveness, many Eastern cultures emphasize indirectness and subtlety. For example, in Japan, it is customary to speak in a more vague and modest manner, using ambiguous expressions referred to as tatemae, to save face and maintain harmony in conversations. By recognizing and adapting to these differences in communication styles, we can foster better understanding and build stronger connections with individuals from different cultural backgrounds. Cultural etiquette also encompasses the understanding and appreciation of taboos and sensitive topics. Each culture has its own set of "red lines", topics that are considered off-limits or taboo. Religious, political, or personal matters related to family and relationships can be particularly sensitive subjects. Being aware of these taboos and avoiding them in conversation helps maintain a respectful and harmonious exchange. As conversationalists, we have a responsibility to avoid perpetuating stereotypes or making assumptions about individuals based on their culture. It is crucial to approach conversations with an open mind, free from biases or prejudices, and to actively listen to the perspectives and experiences of others.

Understanding and respecting cultural etiquette is vital in becoming an effective conversationalist. By familiarizing ourselves with the customs, gestures, and communication styles of different cultures, we can navigate social interactions with sensitivity and respect. This not only ensures that we avoid offending or alienating others but also allows us to foster meaningful connections and create a more inclusive and harmonious society. Embracing cultural diversity and seeking to understand and appreciate each other's differences can enrich our conversations and broaden our horizons. In today's interconnected world, cultural etiquette is not just a matter of politeness; it is a fundamental aspect of being a global citizen and a good conversationalist.

AVOIDING ASSUMPTIONS OR STEREOTYPES

Avoiding assumptions or stereotypes is a key aspect of being a good conversationalist. It is important to approach conversations with an open mind and not make assumptions about others based on their appearance, background, or any preconceived notions. Stereotypes are harmful generalizations that can inhibit meaningful and productive communication. When we assume things about others, we limit our ability to truly understand and appreciate their unique experiences and perspectives. To avoid assumptions, it is crucial to actively listen and engage with others in a non-judgmental manner. This involves suspending our own biases and preconceptions and giving others the opportunity to express themselves freely. In doing so, we can foster an atmosphere of mutual respect and understanding.

One way to avoid assumptions and stereotypes in conversations is to practice empathy. Empathy allows us to put ourselves in someone else's shoes and imagine how they might be feeling or experiencing a situation. By doing this, we can overcome our own biases and gain a deeper understanding of the person we are conversing with. Empathy helps us to respond in a compassionate and sensitive way, which can further enhance the quality of our conversations. Another effective strategy to avoid assumptions is to ask open-ended questions. Open-ended questions encourage the other person to provide more detailed and personal responses, rather than simply answering with a yes or no. By asking open-ended questions, we demonstrate a genuine interest in the other person's thoughts and feelings, which can lead to more meaningful and engaging conversations. Open-ended questions allow us to uncover unique aspects of a person's identity and experiences that may challenge or reshape our own assumptions. It is also important to be aware of our own biases and prejudices. We all possess unconscious biases that influence our perceptions and judgments of others. Acknowledging and challenging these biases is an essential step in avoiding assumptions. By recognizing our own biases, we can actively work towards overcoming them and approaching conversations with a more open and unbiased mindset. This requires self-reflection and a commitment to continuous learning and personal growth. It is crucial to resist the temptation to stereotype others. Stereotypes are oversimplified and often inaccurate generalizations that can unfairly categorize people based on their race, gender, religion, or other characteristics. By avoiding stereotypes, we respect others' individuality and acknowledge the complexity of their identities. Engaging in conversations without resorting to stereotypes allows us to appreciate the diverse perspectives and experiences that others bring to the table. Avoiding assumptions and stereotypes is a fundamental skill in becoming a good conversationalist. By practicing empathy, asking open-ended questions, acknowledging our own biases, and resisting stereotypes, we can create an atmosphere of understanding and respect. Engaging in conversations with an open mind allows us to truly connect with others and build meaningful relationships.

EMBRACING DIVERSITY AND FOSTERING INCLUSIVITY

Diversity encompasses all the differences that exist among individuals, including but not limited to race, ethnicity, gender, sexual orientation, religion, and disability. In a multicultural society, engaging in meaningful conversations requires acknowledging and appreciating the various perspectives and experiences that diversity brings. Being open-minded and receptive to different viewpoints enables us to gain a deeper understanding of others and their lived realities, contributing to a more inclusive and just society. To embrace diversity means to actively seek out opportunities to interact with individuals from different backgrounds and cultures. Engaging in meaningful conversations with people who have different perspectives challenges our own biases and broadens our horizons. By intentionally stepping outside of our comfort zones, we can learn from others' experiences and gain new insights that we may have otherwise overlooked. Inclusivity goes hand in hand with diversity. It is not enough to merely be in the presence of diverse individuals; we must make conscious efforts to ensure that everyone's voices are heard and valued. Inclusive conversations create an environment where individuals from all backgrounds feel comfortable expressing themselves without fear of judgment or marginalization. It is the responsibility of good conversationalists to actively listen to others, validate their experiences, and create a safe space for dialogue. Fostering inclusivity goes beyond individual conversations. It requires systemic change that addresses the structural inequalities and barriers faced by marginalized groups. Embracing diversity and fostering inclusivity means actively advocating for social justice and taking action to dismantle discriminatory practices. This can be achieved through promoting policies that ensure equal opportunities for all, challenging stereotypes and prejudices, and standing up against injustice in all its forms.

Inclusive conversations foster empathy and understanding. When we make an effort to listen to and understand others, we develop a greater sense of empathy towards their experiences. This empathy allows us to connect with others on a deeper level and build stronger relationships. By embracing diversity and fostering inclusivity, we create spaces where individuals feel heard, understood, and valued. The benefits of inclusive conversations extend far beyond personal growth; they contribute to the larger goal of building a more equitable and harmonious society.

Embracing diversity and fostering inclusivity are fundamental aspects of being a good conversationalist. Engaging in meaningful conversations with individuals who possess different perspectives and experiences broadens our understanding and challenges our biases. Actively seeking opportunities to connect with diverse individuals and creating inclusive spaces where everyone's voices are heard and valued is essential. Inclusive conversations foster empathy and understanding, leading to stronger relationships and contributing to a more equitable society. Embracing diversity and fostering inclusivity is not just a personal responsibility, but a collective one that requires ongoing commitment and action.

CELEBRATING DIFFERENCES AS SOURCES OF LEARNING AND ENRICHMENT

In today's diverse society, celebrating differences as sources of learning and enrichment is more important than ever before. By embracing and appreciating the unique perspectives, experiences, and knowledge that individuals from different backgrounds bring to the table, we create an environment that fosters personal growth and intellectual development. When we engage in conversations with people who possess different beliefs, values, and cultures than our own, we open ourselves up to new ways of thinking and expand our understanding of the world around us. This not only leads to an increase in tolerance and empathy but also cultivates critical thinking skills that allow us to challenge our own biases and preconceived notions.

One of the ways in which we can celebrate differences as sources of learning and enrichment is by actively seeking out diverse voices and perspectives. This can be done through engaging in conversations with people who come from different socio-economic backgrounds, ethnicities, and religions. By deliberately reaching out to individuals who have different life experiences than our own, we expose ourselves to alternative viewpoints and broaden our understanding of the world. For example, by having conversations with someone who grew up in poverty, we may gain insights into the challenges they have faced and better understand the systemic issues that contribute to poverty. This awareness can then encourage us to take action to address these inequalities and work towards social justice.

In addition to actively seeking out diverse voices, it is crucial to create an inclusive and respectful environment that encourages individuals to freely express their opinions and experiences. When people feel safe and valued in sharing their perspectives, it enhances the richness of the conversation and allows for a greater exchange of knowledge and ideas. By actively listening to others and being open-minded, we can foster a sense of belonging and create a space where everyone feels heard and respected. This sense of inclusion is essential for encouraging individuals to share their unique insights, which can lead to new discoveries and innovative solutions. Celebrating differences as sources of learning and enrichment involves being willing to challenge our own beliefs and assumptions. By engaging in conversations with individuals who have differing viewpoints, we are forced to confront our own biases and reevaluate our stance on certain issues. This process of self-reflection and critical thinking is essential for personal growth and intellectual development. When we are open to being challenged and are willing to consider alternative perspectives, we become more well-rounded individuals who can navigate complex issues with nuance and empathy. Celebrating differences as sources of learning and enrichment is vital in today's diverse society. By actively seeking out diverse voices, creating an inclusive environment, and challenging our own beliefs, we can foster personal growth, promote empathy, and develop critical thinking skills. These values not only enhance our own lives but contribute to building a more inclusive and equitable society for all.

ENCOURAGING A SAFE AND ACCEPTING ENVIRONMENT FOR ALL PARTICIPANTS

Encouraging a safe and accepting environment for all partici-pants is essential for fostering effective and meaningful conver-sations. In order to create such an environment, it is crucial to establish ground rules that promote respect and openness. Firstly, it is important to emphasize the value of active listening and acknowledging different viewpoints. This can be achieved by encouraging participants to engage in reflective listening, where they paraphrase and summarize the thoughts and feel-ings of others. By doing so, individuals can demonstrate their understanding and show respect for diverse perspectives. Sec-ondly, creating a non-judgmental atmosphere is key to encour-aging open dialogue. Participants should be reminded to sus-pend their biases and preconceived notions, allowing for an un-biased understanding of each other's viewpoints. This can be facilitated by setting guidelines that prohibit personal attacks or derogatory language and promote constructive criticism. By en-suring that all participants feel safe and respected, they will be more likely to contribute to the conversation honestly, thus en-hancing the quality of the discussion. Fostering inclusivity is par-amount to creating a safe and accepting environment. This can be achieved by actively encouraging participation from all indi-viduals and making an effort to include diverse perspectives. By explicitly inviting contributions from marginalized groups or those who may be less vocal, the conversation can become en-riched with a wider range of viewpoints. Facilitators should be sensitive to power dynamics within the conversation and ensure that individuals from different backgrounds have equal opportunities to express themselves. Addressing power imbalances not only promotes fairness but also enhances the overall quality of the dialogue by providing a broader understanding of the topic at hand. It is essential to establish guidelines that protect participants from any form of harassment or discrimination. This can be achieved by explicitly stating a zero-tolerance policy for any behavior that infringes upon an individual's dignity or rights. Setting clear boundaries that prohibit offensive language, personal attacks, or any behavior that perpetuates stereotypes will help maintain a safe and respectful environment for all participants. Establishing mechanisms for reporting instances of harassment or discrimination can provide individuals with the assurance that their concerns will be addressed promptly and effectively. By actively addressing and preventing any form of mistreatment, participants are more likely to feel comfortable expressing their thoughts and ideas freely, leading to a more productive and enriching conversation.

Creating a safe and accepting environment for all participants is crucial for fostering effective and meaningful conversations. By promoting active listening, enhancing inclusivity, and establishing guidelines that prevent harassment or discrimination, individuals can feel respected and valued, leading to a higher quality of dialogue. Encouraging a safe and accepting environment not only enhances the conversation itself but also cultivates a sense of empathy and understanding among participants, enabling them to engage in more productive and empathetic conversations beyond the immediate context.

Being a good conversationalist is an essential skill to have in today's society. Conversations play a crucial role in building personal and professional relationships. Becoming a good conversationalist is not an innate ability; it requires practice and effort. First and foremost, active listening is the key. When engaging in a conversation, one must make a conscious effort to truly listen to the other person's words, rather than simply waiting for their turn to speak. Active listening involves maintaining eye contact, nodding in agreement, and providing verbal and non-verbal cues that show genuine interest. A good conversationalist understands the importance of empathy and tact. It is crucial to put oneself in the other person's shoes and try to understand their perspective and emotions. This shows respect and allows for a more meaningful and harmonious conversation. Being aware of one's own body language is crucial in becoming a good conversationalist. Non-verbal cues such as maintaining an open posture, leaning in slightly towards the speaker, and using appropriate facial expressions can make a conversation more engaging and effective. Using appropriate levels of humor and maintaining a positive attitude are important aspects of being a good conversationalist. A well-timed, tasteful joke can lighten the mood and make the conversation more enjoyable. It is imperative to gauge the other person's reaction and ensure that humor is used in a respectful manner. Maintaining a positive attitude during a conversation can help create a welcoming and friendly atmosphere. Another aspect of being a good conversationalist is being knowledgeable on a wide range of topics. This allows for more meaningful and interesting discussions. By broadening one's knowledge base and staying informed about current events, cultural topics, and various areas of interest, one can contribute more to conversations and engage the other person with interesting insights and perspectives. On a similar note, asking open-ended questions is an effective way to keep a conversation flowing and show a genuine interest in the other person. Open-ended questions invite the speaker to expand on their thoughts and provide more detailed responses, fostering a deeper connection between both parties. It is important to recognize that being a good conversationalist is not about dominating the conversation, but rather creating a balanced dialogue. Allowing the other person to speak uninterrupted and giving them the space to express their thoughts and feelings is crucial. Interrupting or monopolizing the conversation can lead to misunderstandings and hinder the building of a meaningful connection. Becoming a good conversationalist requires active listening, empathy, awareness of body language, appropriate humor, a positive attitude, knowledge on various topics, asking open-ended questions, and creating a balanced dialogue. These skills can be developed through practice and effort, and with time, one can become a highly skilled conversationalist, capable of fostering deep and meaningful connections with others.

XV. NAVIGATING DIFFICULT CONVERSATIONS

Navigating difficult conversations is a necessary skill that every good conversationalist should possess. These conversations can range from discussions involving sensitive topics to debates with opposing viewpoints. In order to navigate these conversations effectively, one must first recognize the importance of empathy and openness. It is crucial to approach these discussions with a willingness to listen and understand the perspective of the other person. This requires setting aside one's own biases and preconceived notions, allowing room for meaningful dialogue to take place. One key aspect of navigating difficult conversations is choosing the right words. Words have the power to either escalate or defuse tensions, and it is essential to use them wisely. The use of inclusive language, avoiding derogatory terms or stereotypes, can foster an environment of respect and understanding. Employing active listening skills, such as asking clarifying questions and paraphrasing the other person's points, can ensure that both parties feel heard and validated.

Another important skill in navigating difficult conversations is managing emotions. These discussions can often be emotionally charged, and it is imperative not to let emotions hijack the conversation. Remaining calm, composed, and respectful, even in the face of provocation, sets an example for others and promotes healthy discourse. Emotions should not be dismissed, but rather acknowledged and addressed in a constructive and empathetic manner. Having a mindset of collaboration rather than confrontation can greatly contribute to navigating difficult conversations. Approaching these discussions with the intention of finding common ground and working towards a solution allows for a more productive exchange of ideas. It is important to remember that the goal is not to win an argument, but rather to gain a deeper understanding and potentially reach a resolution that satisfies both parties. In addition to the aforementioned skills, recognizing and acknowledging one's own biases is essential in navigating difficult conversations. We all have our own perspectives shaped by our experiences, beliefs, and cultural backgrounds, which can sometimes cloud our judgement or influence our reactions. Taking the time to reflect on these biases and being willing to challenge and expand our own worldview is a vital step towards fostering inclusivity and understanding in conversations. Navigating difficult conversations requires a willingness to be vulnerable. Sharing personal stories or experiences can create connections and promote empathy. By opening oneself up in a respectful and authentic way, it encourages others to do the same, leading to deeper and more meaningful conversations. Navigating difficult conversations is an indispensable skill that every good conversationalist must cultivate. It involves employing empathy and openness, choosing the right words, managing emotions, fostering a collaborative mindset, recognizing biases, and being willing to be vulnerable. By honing these skills and approaching difficult conversations with respect and a genuine desire to understand, individuals can become adept at navigating challenging discussions and fostering healthy and enlightening dialogue.

MAINTAINING COMPOSURE AND RESPECT

When engaged in a conversation, it is essential to stay composed and maintain respectful behavior. Composure plays a vital role in the success of a conversation, as maintaining a calm demeanor allows one to think clearly and express oneself effectively. Losing composure during a conversation can result in the deterioration of the conversation, leading to misunderstandings or conflicts. Respect is another critical component for a positive conversation. Respecting both oneself and the other person involved in the conversation fosters a healthy exchange of ideas and opinions. By respecting others, one demonstrates empathy and understanding, which in turn encourages openness and willingness for the other person to reciprocate. Maintaining respect ensures that all parties feel valued and heard. When individuals feel respected, they are more likely to actively engage in the conversation as they feel safe expressing their thoughts and feelings. Maintaining composure and respect also involves being mindful of one's tone and body language. The tone of voice can greatly impact the outcome of a conversation. Speaking in a calm and composed tone helps convey a sense of reason and level-headedness, promoting a respectful and constructive exchange of ideas. Being conscious of body language is crucial, as it not only affects how others perceive us but also influences how we ourselves feel during the conversation. A relaxed and open stance can help establish a positive and inviting atmosphere, while the avoidance of aggressive or defensive body language prevents the conversation from becoming confrontational or hostile. Maintaining composure and respect also involves actively listening to the other person. Active listening is the ability to fully absorb and understand what the other person is saying, without interrupting or judgment. By actively listening, one shows respect for the other person's perspectives, experiences, and opinions, which encourages a more meaningful and productive conversation. Active listening allows individuals to respond thoughtfully and appropriately, as it provides them with a comprehensive understanding of the topic at hand. Maintaining composure and respect are vital skills for being a good conversationalist. By staying composed, individuals can think clearly and express themselves effectively. Respect, both for oneself and the other person, fosters a healthy exchange of ideas and encourages active engagement in the conversation. Being mindful of one's tone and body language creates a positive and inviting atmosphere, preventing conflicts or misunderstandings. Active listening enables individuals to fully understand and respond appropriately to the conversation. Individuals who possess composure and respect contribute to meaningful and constructive conversations that foster understanding and connection.

KEEPING EMOTIONS IN CHECK DURING CHALLENGING DISCUSSIONS

This is a vital skill for individuals striving to become effective conversationalists. When engaged in conversations that involve sensitive or controversial topics, emotions can run high, potentially hindering meaningful exchanges and limiting the possibility of reaching mutually satisfactory resolutions. Recognizing the importance of emotional regulation in these circumstances requires one to understand the impact that unchecked emotions can have on the overall tone and outcome of a conversation.

Ensuring emotions are kept in check begins with self-awareness—a critical aspect of emotional intelligence. Being aware of our own emotional triggers and personal biases can help us anticipate and manage our emotional responses when faced with challenging discussions. This level of self-awareness allows individuals to actively monitor their emotions throughout the conversation, preventing them from escalating towards an unproductive or confrontational state. In addition to self-awareness, maintaining emotional control during challenging discussions involves developing the skills necessary to respond rather than react. Reacting impulsively to strong emotions can lead to counterproductive behaviors, such as interrupting, raising one's voice, or becoming defensive. Conversely, responding thoughtfully allows individuals to navigate these discussions with greater empathy, open-mindedness, and respect for differing viewpoints. By taking a moment to reflect before responding, individuals can better regulate their emotions, promote constructive dialogue, and cultivate a positive conversational environment.

Another fruitful approach for keeping emotions in check involves actively practicing active listening. Active listening entails not only hearing the words of the speaker but also making an effort to comprehend their underlying message, perspective, and emotions. By fully understanding the speaker's viewpoint, individuals can suppress their own emotional reactions and approach the discussion from a place of empathy and understanding. This empathetic stance can foster a more productive and respectful conversation, reducing the likelihood of emotional outbursts or misunderstandings. The ability to keep emotions in check does not imply suppressing or invalidating one's emotions altogether. Emotions are integral to human nature, and acknowledging their presence during challenging discussions can contribute to a genuine and authentic exchange. Instead of suppressing emotions, individuals should strive to express them in a constructive manner, using "I" statements to convey their feelings and concerns without attacking or belittling others. This assertive approach allows them to present their perspectives while maintaining emotional balance and keeping the conversation focused on the topic at hand. Keeping emotions in check during challenging discussions is essential for those who seek to become effective conversationalists. By cultivating self-awareness, practicing emotional control, actively listening, and expressing emotions constructively, individuals can navigate these conversations with greater empathy, respect, and understanding. The ability to regulate emotions allows for a more fruitful exchange of ideas, facilitates problem-solving, and fosters stronger relationships built on open and honest communication.

Developing this skill requires ongoing practice and self-reflection, but the rewards in terms of personal growth and improved conversational abilities are well worth the effort.

FOSTERING A CONSTRUCTIVE ATMOSPHERE FOR DISAGREEMENT

In order to be a good conversationalist, one must possess the ability to foster a constructive atmosphere for disagreement. This entails creating an environment where individuals feel comfortable expressing diverging opinions without fear of judgment or animosity. Open dialogue and respectful communication are key elements in nurturing this type of atmosphere. Firstly, it is essential to approach conversations with an open mind and willingness to listen to alternative viewpoints. This means suspending judgment and striving to understand the underlying reasoning behind others' opinions. By doing so, one can demonstrate empathy and respect towards differing viewpoints, ultimately fostering a constructive atmosphere. Active listening plays a vital role in creating an environment conducive to disagreement. This involves concentrating on the speaker's words, non-verbal cues, and tone of voice, thus indicating genuine interest and attentiveness. By actively listening, one can ensure that they fully comprehend the other person's perspective, leading to a more informed and thoughtful response. Validating others' opinions is crucial for maintaining a constructive atmosphere during conversations. Validating does not necessarily mean agreeing, but rather acknowledging the validity of someone's viewpoint and recognizing their right to hold it. By validating others, we convey respect and foster an environment where disagreement is seen as an opportunity for growth rather than a threat. It is essential to respond to disagreement with assertiveness rather than aggression. Assertiveness involves expressing one's own perspective clearly and confidently without insulting or belittling others. By maintaining a calm and respectful demeanor, one can encourage healthy debate and facilitate the exchange of differing ideas. Recognizing common ground is instrumental in creating a constructive atmosphere for disagreement. Finding shared values or goals can serve as a basis for building bridges between conflicting viewpoints. This can help reduce hostility and promote a more collaborative approach towards resolving disagreements. It is crucial to embrace the concept of intellectual humility in fostering a constructive atmosphere for disagreement. Intellectual humility involves recognizing the limits of one's knowledge and being open to revising one's beliefs based on new evidence or persuasive arguments. By acknowledging our fallibility, we create an environment that values learning and growth over stubbornness and self-righteousness. Fostering a constructive atmosphere for disagreement requires a combination of open-mindedness, active listening, validation, assertiveness, recognition of common ground, and intellectual humility. By implementing these strategies, individuals can engage in meaningful conversations that promote mutual understanding and personal growth. It is through these constructive interactions that we can broaden our perspectives and contribute to the collective advancement of knowledge and society.

SEEKING COMMON GROUND AND COMPROMISE

In any conversation, it is inevitable that people will have different perspectives, opinions, and ideas. Instead of focusing on these differences and arguing, a good conversationalist actively seeks common ground and attempts to find a compromise. This is important because it allows for a deeper and more meaningful conversation, where both parties feel heard and valued. Seeking common ground and compromise helps to build stronger connections and relationships. When individuals are able to find common ground, they are more likely to develop a mutual understanding and respect for one another. This not only enhances the conversation but also strengthens the bond between the participants. Seeking common ground and compromise fosters open-mindedness and intellectual growth. By exposing oneself to different perspectives and ideas, individuals can expand their own knowledge and challenge their preconceived notions. It promotes critical thinking and encourages individuals to consider alternative views, which ultimately leads to personal and intellectual development. Seeking common ground and compromise contributes to the resolution of conflicts. In many instances, conflicts arise from misunderstandings or differences in opinions. By actively seeking common ground and being open to compromise, individuals can defuse tense situations and find a resolution that satisfies all parties involved. This is particularly significant in relationships, whether personal or professional, where conflicts can be detrimental if not addressed properly. Seeking common ground and compromise facilitates effective teamwork and collaboration. In any group setting, individuals may come from diverse backgrounds and have contrasting ideas. By actively seeking common ground and being willing to compromise, a group can effectively work together towards a shared goal. This ability to find common ground and compromise not only enhances the group's productivity but also creates a positive and harmonious working environment. Seeking common ground and compromise is a crucial aspect of being a good conversationalist. It allows for meaningful conversations, builds stronger connections and relationships, fosters open-mindedness and intellectual growth, contributes to conflict resolution, and facilitates effective teamwork and collaboration. Seeking common ground and compromise not only benefits the individual but also cultivates a more inclusive and harmonious society. It is of utmost importance to actively practice and develop this skill in order to become a good conversationalist and contribute positively to personal and collective growth.

IDENTIFYING SHARED GOALS OR VALUES

In order to be a good conversationalist, it is crucial to identify and understand shared goals or values between individuals. This concept is based on the fundamental idea that effective communication requires mutual understanding and common ground. Identifying shared goals or values allows for meaningful conversations to take place, as it provides a framework for individuals to connect and relate to one another. When engaging in a conversation, it is important to actively listen and observe the other person's words and actions in order to gauge their goals or values. This can be accomplished by paying close attention to the language they use, the topics they choose to discuss, and the emotions they convey. By doing so, one can gain insight into the other person's beliefs, ideals, and priorities. Identifying shared goals or values promotes an environment of trust and openness, which fosters more authentic and engaging conversations.

Identifying shared goals or values also allows for the creation of a sense of common purpose, leading to stronger and more meaningful connections. When individuals discover that they share similar aspirations or principles, they are more likely to connect on a deeper level and invest in the conversation. This mutual understanding encourages individuals to support and collaborate with one another, fostering a greater sense of cooperation and teamwork. Whether it is in a personal or professional context, shared goals or values provide a foundation for individuals to work towards a common objective. For instance, in a professional setting, colleagues who share the same vision for success are more likely to collaborate effectively, resulting in increased productivity and innovation. Similarly, in a personal context, identifying shared goals or values can strengthen relationships by creating a sense of unity and shared purpose.

Recognizing shared goals or values can also play a role in conflict resolution. When individuals find themselves in a disagreement or debate, acknowledging common ground can serve as a starting point for finding a solution. By focusing on shared goals or values, individuals can shift the conversation away from personal differences and towards a shared commitment to finding common ground. This approach allows individuals to address their concerns in a constructive and respectful manner, facilitating the resolution of conflicts. By emphasizing shared goals or values, individuals are more likely to find common solutions and develop a greater understanding and empathy for one another. Identifying shared goals or values is a crucial aspect of being a good conversationalist. It promotes mutual understanding, cultivates stronger connections, and facilitates conflict resolution. By actively listening and observing, individuals can gain insight into the beliefs and priorities of others. Recognizing shared goals or values allows for the creation of a sense of common purpose and unity, which leads to more meaningful conversations and collaborations. Whether in personal or professional settings, identifying shared goals or values lays the groundwork for successful communication and fosters stronger relationships.

COLLABORATING TO FIND MUTUALLY BENEFICIAL SOLUTIONS

Collaborating to find mutually beneficial solutions is an essential aspect of being a good conversationalist. In any conversation, especially those involving complex or contentious topics, it is crucial to approach the discussion with an open mind and a willingness to find common ground. By fostering an environment of collaboration, individuals can work together to seek solutions that satisfy the interests and needs of all parties involved. This approach requires active listening and empathy as conversationalists must put themselves in the shoes of others to truly understand their perspectives and concerns. Collaborating to find mutually beneficial solutions also involves recognizing and valuing divergent opinions. In a diverse and pluralistic society, it is inevitable that individuals will have different viewpoints and beliefs. Rather than dismissing or shutting down these perspectives, a good conversationalist appreciates the diversity of thought and uses it as an opportunity for learning and growth. By welcoming differing opinions, individuals can engage in a more enriching and productive conversation that enables them to uncover alternative perspectives and potential solutions. Collaborating to find mutually beneficial solutions requires effective communication and problem-solving skills. During a conversation, it is common for disagreements or conflicts to arise, requiring conversationalists to navigate these challenges in a constructive manner. This involves maintaining a respectful tone, refraining from personal attacks, and focusing on addressing the issue at hand rather than engaging in unnecessary tangents. By prioritizing the resolution of the problem rather than winning an argument or asserting one's dominance, conversationalists can create an atmosphere conducive to collaboration. Effective communication entails not only conveying one's ideas clearly and succinctly but also actively seeking clarification and feedback from others. By engaging in dialogue and seeking input from others, individuals can foster a sense of ownership and shared responsibility for finding mutually beneficial solutions. Collaborating to find mutually beneficial solutions necessitates a willingness to compromise and find common ground. It is improbable that all parties will achieve their ideal outcome in every conversation, especially ones involving conflicting interests. Good conversationalists understand the importance of flexible thinking and making concessions to reach a mutually satisfactory resolution. This requires recognizing that one's own perspective may not be the only valid one and being willing to adapt one's position based on new information or insights gained during the course of the conversation. The ability to collaborate to find mutually beneficial solutions is a crucial skill for being a good conversationalist. By fostering an environment of collaboration, valuing divergent opinions, practicing effective communication, and being willing to compromise, individuals can engage in productive conversations that lead to constructive outcomes. This collaborative approach not only enhances personal relationships but also contributes to the development of a more inclusive and harmonious society. Developing good conversational skills is an essential aspect of successful human interaction. In a world where constant communication is a necessity, being able to engage in conversations effectively can lead to numerous benefits. To become a good conversationalist, one must cultivate active listening skills, display genuine interest in others, and maintain a positive attitude during conversations. Active listening involves fully focusing on the speaker, absorbing their words, and responding appropriately. When someone is actively listening, they can understand the speaker's perspective and offer meaningful contributions, fostering a sense of connection and respect. Showing genuine interest in others can make conversations more engaging and enjoyable. By asking thought-provoking questions, seeking to understand others' opinions, and demonstrating empathy, one can create an atmosphere conducive to fruitful discussions. Demonstrating curiosity about others' experiences also helps in making people feel valued and validated, which encourages open and honest communication. Maintaining a positive attitude is vital in any conversation. Positivity not only puts others at ease but also creates a pleasant environment for dialogue. A warm and friendly approach helps to establish rapport and encourages others to be more open in expressing their thoughts and feelings. Maintaining a positive attitude also involves refraining from judgment and criticism, as it can discourage individuals from participating in meaningful conversations. Becoming a good conversationalist involves honing active listening skills, displaying genuine interest in others, and maintaining a positive attitude throughout conversations.

Body language plays a crucial role in effective communication. Nonverbal cues often convey emotions and intentions more powerfully than words alone. To be a good conversationalist, it is essential to be aware of one's own body language and remain vigilant to others' nonverbal signals. Maintaining eye contact with the speaker demonstrates attentiveness and interest. Conversely, avoiding eye contact can signal disinterest or discomfort. Posture and hand gestures reflect engagement in a conversation. Sitting up straight and leaning slightly forward conveys interest and receptiveness. Conversely, slouched posture and crossed arms may signal defensiveness or indifference. Mirroring the body language of the speaker, within reason, can also help establish rapport and create a sense of connection. Conversely, mismatched body language can make conversation feel disconnected or strained. Being mindful of nonverbal cues and adapting one's own body language appropriately can greatly enhance conversational skills. Developing good conversational skills is crucial for effective communication. Active listening, displaying genuine interest, maintaining a positive attitude, and being aware of body language are all key components of becoming a good conversationalist. Engaging in meaningful conversations not only facilitates understanding and empathy but also fosters the building of strong relationships. By continuously practicing and refining these skills, individuals can improve their conversational abilities and enjoy more fulfilling interactions with others.

XVI.   PRACTICE, FEEDBACK, AND REFLECTION

To become a skilled conversationalist, one must continually engage in practice, seek feedback, and engage in reflection. Without intentional practice, improvement is unlikely. Practicing conversational skills can involve a wide range of activities, such as participating in group discussions, engaging in debates, and even role-playing various conversational scenarios. By actively participating in these activities, individuals can develop their ability to comprehend and articulate ideas effectively. Seeking feedback from trusted sources, such as friends, family, or mentors, can provide valuable insights into areas for improvement. Constructive criticism can help individuals identify their strengths and weaknesses, enabling them to focus their efforts on specific areas requiring development. Receiving feedback allows individuals to gain a fresh perspective on their conversational style and adapt accordingly. Reflection is an integral part of the learning process, as it allows individuals to analyze past conversations, identifying points of success and areas in need of improvement. Reflecting on one's conversational skills can involve pondering upon the effectiveness of different approaches taken, considering the nonverbal cues given, and evaluating the impact of specific words or phrases used. By reflecting on past experiences, individuals can identify patterns and tendencies, enabling them to make conscious choices about their conversational style in the future. It is important to understand that improving conversational skills is an ongoing process that requires continuous practice, feedback, and reflection. Even the most skilled conversationalists can still encounter challenges or areas in need of improvement. It is vital to remain open to feedback and adaptable to change throughout the conversational journey. Embracing a growth mindset, individuals can view feedback and constructive criticism as opportunities for growth rather than as personal attacks. Consistently engaging in self-reflection can help individuals uncover their own biases, prejudices, or communication barriers that may hinder effective conversation. By addressing these personal limitations, individuals can cultivate a more inclusive and empathetic conversational style that fosters meaningful dialogue. Becoming a good conversationalist requires deliberate effort and commitment. By continuously practicing, seeking feedback, and engaging in reflection, individuals can enhance their conversational skills and become more effective communicators. Through intentional practice, individuals can polish their ability to express their thoughts clearly and eloquently. Seeking feedback from trusted sources allows individuals to gain valuable insights and identify areas for improvement. Reflection enables individuals to evaluate their conversational style, identifying patterns, and tendencies that may influence their interactions. By engaging in these three practices, individuals can cultivate their conversational skills, foster meaningful dialogue, and navigate various social and professional settings with confidence and ease.

ENGAGING IN REGULAR CONVERSATIONAL PRACTICE

Engaging in regular conversational practice is crucial for developing effective communication skills and becoming a good conversationalist. The ability to engage in meaningful conversations is not only essential for personal and social interactions but also beneficial for academic and professional success. Regular practice allows individuals to gradually improve their conversational abilities by refining their verbal and non-verbal communication skills, expanding their vocabulary, and developing active listening skills. Firstly, engaging in regular conversational practice helps individuals refine their verbal and non-verbal communication skills. Through practice, individuals become more comfortable expressing their thoughts and ideas effectively, allowing them to engage in conversations with confidence. Regular conversational practice enables individuals to experiment with different communication techniques, such as using appropriate body language, maintaining eye contact, and using gestures to enhance their message. As individuals practice conversing, they gain an understanding of how their words and actions can impact the overall conversation and the individuals they are communicating with. Secondly, regular conversational practice allows individuals to expand their vocabulary. Engaging in conversations with different people exposes individuals to various perspectives and ideas, leading to a wider range of vocabulary acquisition. Through conversation, individuals are constantly challenged to articulate their thoughts using precise and effective language, which in turn enhances their communication skills. Engaging in regular conversational practice provides individuals with opportunities to learn new words and phrases, allowing them to vary their language use and express themselves more effectively. Regular conversational practice helps individuals develop active listening skills. Engaging in conversations requires not only speaking but also actively listening to others. By practicing listening attentively, individuals become more skilled at understanding and interpreting the speaker's message. Through active listening, individuals are able to respond appropriately, ask relevant questions, and participate actively in the conversation. Regular conversational practice helps individuals develop empathy, as they learn to attentively listen to others' feelings and experiences, fostering deeper connections and more meaningful conversations. Engaging in regular conversational practice is essential for developing effective communication skills and becoming a good conversationalist. Through practice, individuals refine their verbal and non-verbal communication skills, expand their vocabulary, and develop active listening abilities. By actively participating in conversations, individuals gain confidence and become more skilled at expressing their thoughts and ideas. Regular conversational practice exposes individuals to different perspectives and ideas, expanding their vocabulary and language use. Practicing active listening enhances individuals' ability to understand and interpret the messages of others, leading to more meaningful and engaging conversations. Thus, investing time in regular conversational practice is beneficial for personal, social, academic, and professional growth.

PARTICIPATING IN GROUP DISCUSSIONS OR DEBATES

Participating in group discussions or debates is an essential skill that contributes to becoming a good conversationalist. Engaging in such interactions allows individuals to challenge their own perspectives, learn from others, and foster a sense of community. Group discussions provide a platform for individuals to share their ideas, opinions, and knowledge on a particular topic. This exchange of thoughts stimulates critical thinking, as individuals are exposed to diverse viewpoints and are encouraged to analyze and evaluate various arguments. By actively participating in group discussions, one develops the ability to articulate their ideas coherently and persuasively, which is crucial for effective communication. Engaging in debates enables individuals to practice the art of persuasion and logical reasoning, enhancing their ability to present convincing arguments. These skills are especially valuable in academic settings, where students are often required to express their thoughts through presentations, seminars, or group projects.

Group discussions and debates serve an important purpose in fostering a sense of community. By bringing together individuals with different backgrounds, experiences, and perspectives, these interactions create an environment where individuals can connect and engage with one another. Through active participation, individuals can develop empathy, understanding, and respect for diverse opinions. This sense of community not only enhances the quality of conversations but also cultivates a healthy learning environment where everyone feels valued and appreciated.

Participating in group discussions or debates also plays a crucial role in personal growth and self-improvement. Engaging with others allows individuals to challenge their own beliefs and expand their knowledge base. By being open to alternative viewpoints, individuals are exposed to new ideas and different ways of thinking, broadening their horizons. This exposure to diverse perspectives nurtures intellectual growth and curiosity, enabling individuals to view the world through multiple lenses. Group discussions and debates can help individuals develop crucial skills such as active listening, critical thinking, and effective communication, which are transferable to various aspects of life beyond the realm of conversation. Participating in group discussions or debates is a fundamental aspect of becoming a good conversationalist. These interactions provide opportunities to challenge one's own perspectives, learn from others, and foster a sense of community. By actively engaging in such discussions, individuals enhance their ability to articulate ideas persuasively, practice logical reasoning, and develop critical thinking skills. These interactions promote personal growth, self-improvement, and the formation of meaningful connections. By actively participating in group discussions or debates, individuals can become well-rounded conversationalists who are capable of engaging in thought-provoking conversations, understanding diverse perspectives, and contributing to a thriving intellectual community.

SEEKING OPPORTUNITIES TO ENGAGE WITH DIVERSE INDIVIDUALS

One important aspect of being a good conversationalist is seeking opportunities to engage with diverse individuals. While it may be comfortable to stick to conversations with people who share similar backgrounds and viewpoints as ourselves, it is essential to step out of our comfort zones and interact with individuals from diverse backgrounds. Engaging with diverse individuals allows us to broaden our perspectives and challenge our own biases and assumptions. This leads to personal growth and a more inclusive worldview. Conversing with people from different walks of life opens doors to learning about new cultures, beliefs, and experiences that we may have been unaware of otherwise. This knowledge enriches our conversations and enables us to engage with others in a more respectful and meaningful manner. Seeking opportunities to engage with diverse individuals can be accomplished in various ways. One effective strategy is to actively participate in diverse social activities, such as joining clubs and organizations that promote diversity and inclusion. These groups often provide a platform for individuals from different backgrounds to come together, facilitating meaningful conversations and opportunities for learning. Attending cultural events and festivals allows us to immerse ourselves in different traditions and customs, providing valuable insights into other cultures and fostering a greater appreciation for diversity. In addition to seeking out diverse social activities, it is important to approach conversations with an open mind and genuine curiosity about others' perspectives. Active listening is crucial in fostering dialogue and understanding. By truly listening to what others have to say and suspending judgment, we can create a safe space for individuals to express themselves freely. This not only encourages a healthy exchange of ideas but also promotes empathy and understanding.

Seeking opportunities to engage with diverse individuals goes hand in hand with developing effective communication skills. Being a good conversationalist involves not only expressing ourselves clearly but also acknowledging and valuing the thoughts and opinions of others. By practicing empathetic communication, we can ensure that everyone feels heard and respected, fostering an atmosphere of inclusivity and openness. This can be achieved through techniques such as active listening, asking open-ended questions, and showing genuine interest in the other person's experiences and ideas. Actively seeking opportunities to engage with diverse individuals is a vital component of being a good conversationalist. By stepping out of our comfort zones and interacting with people from different backgrounds, we broaden our perspectives, challenge our biases, and promote inclusivity. Engaging in diverse social activities, attending cultural events, and approaching conversations with an open mind and empathy are effective strategies in fostering meaningful connections with individuals from diverse backgrounds. Embracing diversity in our conversations not only enhances our personal growth but also contributes to a more inclusive and understanding society.

SEEKING FEEDBACK TO IMPROVE CONVERSATIONAL SKILLS

In order to become a good conversationalist, seeking feedback is crucial for improving one's conversational skills. Feedback plays a pivotal role in identifying areas that require improvement and allows individuals to gain valuable insights into their communication style. When we engage in conversations, we may sometimes overlook certain aspects of our interpersonal communication that can hinder the fluidity of our dialogues. Actively seeking feedback from others can help us gain a deeper understanding of our conversational strengths and weaknesses.

Firstly, seeking feedback from others can help individuals identify areas where they may need improvement. Sometimes, we may unintentionally interrupt others or dominate the conversation, preventing others from expressing their thoughts effectively. By seeking feedback on our conversational skills, we can identify these patterns and take steps to rectify them. For instance, a friend or family member can point out that we tend to interrupt others without even realizing it. This feedback can prompt us to reflect on our conversational habits and work towards becoming better listeners. By opening ourselves up to constructive criticism, we can gain insights into aspects of our communication that may hinder our conversational skills and subsequently work towards addressing them.

Seeking feedback provides valuable insights into our communication style that we may be unaware of. Each person has their own unique communication style influenced by their upbringing, cultural background, and personal experiences. Seeking feedback from others allows us to understand how others perceive our communication style, which can help us adjust our approach to various social and professional settings. For example, a co-worker may provide feedback on our tendency to use overly formal language in casual conversations, which might create a barrier in building a rapport with others. Being receptive to this feedback enables us to adapt our communication style accordingly, fostering more effective and engaging conversations.

Seeking feedback on our conversational skills can assist in our personal growth and development. Accepting feedback without defensiveness and making efforts to improve based on this feedback demonstrates open-mindedness and a willingness to grow as individuals. By actively seeking feedback, we display a genuine interest in honing our conversational skills, which can shape us into more empathetic, understanding, and engaging individuals. This personal growth positively impacts not only our communication skills but also our overall ability to connect with others on a deeper level. Seeking feedback is indispensable for enhancing one's conversational skills. By actively seeking feedback, individuals can identify areas that need improvement, gain insights into their communication style, and experience personal growth. Feedback serves as a valuable tool for self-reflection, enabling us to become better listeners, adjust our communication style, and foster more meaningful connections with others. By embracing feedback and working towards improvement, we can become adept conversationalists who can engage in fulfilling and enriching dialogues.

RECEIVING CONSTRUCTIVE CRITICISM FROM TRUSTED PEERS

One of the most valuable skills a good conversationalist must possess is the ability to receive and embrace constructive criticism from trusted peers. Constructive criticism provides an opportunity for personal growth and development. By actively seeking out feedback from individuals we trust and respect, we open ourselves up to invaluable insights and suggestions that can help us improve our conversational skills. It is important to remember that we should only seek feedback from those we trust, as their opinions will be honest, objective, and genuinely helpful. Constructive criticism allows us to identify areas of improvement that we may not have been aware of ourselves. By listening and acknowledging the feedback given to us, we can learn from our mistakes, refine our conversational techniques, and ultimately become better communicators. Receiving constructive criticism from trusted peers demonstrates humility and the willingness to learn. It shows that we value the opinions and perspectives of others and are open to continuous personal and professional growth. When we actively seek feedback from our peers, we create an environment of mutual respect and support, where everyone can contribute to each other's improvement. Receiving constructive criticism from trusted peers helps to foster stronger relationships. It allows for open and honest communication, as well as the opportunity to address any misunderstandings or areas of tension. When we are receptive to feedback, it shows that we value the relationship and are willing to work on ourselves to maintain and strengthen it. Trust is built when peers see that we take their opinions seriously and are committed to personal development. Embracing constructive criticism can lead to increased self-awareness. When we evaluate our conversational skills through the lens of others, we gain a better understanding of how our behaviors may be perceived by others. This self-awareness enables us to make conscious changes in our communication style, allowing us to adapt to different situations and audiences. It also helps us become more mindful of our words, tone, and body language, ensuring that our conversations are respectful, inclusive, and engaging. Receiving constructive criticism from trusted peers is essential for personal growth, relationship building, and self-awareness. By actively seeking out feedback, we create an environment of learning and improvement, where everyone can contribute to the development of effective conversational skills. It is important to approach feedback with an open mind and a willingness to learn from our mistakes. Constructive criticism allows us to identify areas of improvement we may have overlooked and helps us become better communicators. Embracing feedback from trusted peers not only benefits our personal growth but also strengthens the relationships we have with those around us.

REFLECTING ON AREAS OF IMPROVEMENT AND SETTING GOALS

In order to continually develop and enhance our conversational skills, it is essential to identify the areas in which we may be lacking and determine specific goals to overcome these deficiencies. One area that often requires improvement is active listening. Many individuals tend to focus on formulating their response or waiting for their turn to speak rather than genuinely listening to the speaker. This hinders effective communication and can lead to misinterpretation or misunderstandings. An important goal for a conversationalist would be to actively listen, offering undivided attention to the speaker, and responding thoughtfully based on the content discussed. Another area for improvement is non-verbal communication. Body language, facial expressions, and gestures all play a significant role in conveying our thoughts and feelings during conversations. Individuals may struggle with maintaining appropriate eye contact, using open and welcoming body language, or regulating their facial expressions. Recognizing these deficiencies and setting a goal to improve non-verbal communication can help create a more engaging and inclusive conversation environment. Understanding the importance of empathy and perspective-taking is essential in order to be a good conversationalist. Empathy enables individuals to connect with others on a deeper level, demonstrating that they genuinely care about the speaker's thoughts and emotions. By setting a goal to practice empathy, individuals can work towards becoming more attuned to the needs and feelings of others, fostering a more compassionate and understanding conversation. Alongside empathy, perspective-taking allows us to see a conversation from different angles, considering the speaker's viewpoints and providing a more well-rounded response. Making an effort to enhance perspective-taking skills by setting specific goals, such as actively seeking differing opinions or engaging in diverse conversations, can contribute to becoming a better conversationalist. A crucial aspect of self-improvement in conversational skills is self-reflection. Taking the time to evaluate past conversations can provide insight into the areas that require improvement and inform future goal setting. By examining one's own contributions to a conversation, individuals can identify any patterns of behavior that may hinder effective communication, such as interrupting or dominating the discussion. These observations can then be used to set goals focused on maintaining a balanced and respectful conversational dynamic. Reflecting on areas of improvement and setting goals is instrumental in the journey towards becoming a good conversationalist. By identifying specific areas for enhancement, such as active listening, non-verbal communication, empathy, perspective-taking, and self-reflection, individuals can embark on a path of continual growth in their conversational skills. This self-awareness and commitment to improvement can allow for more fulfilling and meaningful conversations, fostering stronger connections with others and promoting effective communication in various personal and professional settings. In the bustling world we live in, the art of conversation often takes a backseat to the omnipresence of technology and the fast-paced nature of our lives. Honing one's conversational skills can greatly enhance the quality of our interactions and foster meaningful connections with others. The ability to engage in meaningful conversations is not only a valuable skill in social settings but also in academic and professional contexts. Excellent conversationalists possess certain qualities and techniques that contribute to successful exchanges. First and foremost, active listening is crucial for effective communication. This involves fully engaging with the speaker's words, understanding their perspective, and responding appropriately. Active listeners demonstrate empathy and provide verbal and non-verbal cues to indicate their attentiveness. They listen with genuine curiosity and seek to comprehend the speaker's message rather than just waiting for their turn to speak. Another essential aspect of being a good conversationalist is the ability to ask thought-provoking and open-ended questions. By posing questions that invite further reflection and discussion, conversationalists encourage the speaker to delve deeper into their thoughts and ideas. Such questions demonstrate an interest in the other person's perspective and stimulate intellectual engagement. Avoiding interruptions and allowing the speaker to express their thoughts uninterrupted is key to fostering a respectful and productive conversation. It is important to remember that conversation should be a two-way street, where both parties have the opportunity to speak and be heard. Alongside active listening and asking thought-provoking questions, good conversationalists utilize body language to convey their engagement. Maintaining eye contact, nodding in agreement or understanding, and using appropriate facial expressions are all examples of non-verbal cues that signal attentiveness and interest. Considerate interruptions and turn-taking are crucial components of a successful conversation. Demonstrating respect for the speaker's words by allowing them to have their uninterrupted say fosters a comfortable environment of trust and understanding. Beyond these techniques, being knowledgeable about a variety of subjects can greatly enhance one's conversational skills. Having a broad range of interests and staying up-to-date with current events ensures that conversations have a diverse and intellectually stimulating nature. Expressing genuine enthusiasm and passion for the topic at hand can be infectious, motivating the other person to engage more actively in the conversation. Maintaining a positive and non-judgmental attitude is an essential quality of a good conversationalist. This involves refraining from criticism or belittlement and instead fostering an environment of acceptance and understanding. By embodying these qualities and techniques, one can truly become a good conversationalist, capable of fostering meaningful connections and expanding their knowledge through fruitful exchanges. The art of conversation is an important skill to cultivate in today's fast-paced world. Active listening, asking thought-provoking questions, utilizing body language, maintaining knowledge on various subjects, and having a positive attitude are all essential components of being a good conversationalist. By practicing these skills, we can enrich our interactions and create meaningful connections with others.

XVII. CONCLUSION

Being a good conversationalist is an essential skill that can greatly enhance one's personal and professional life. By considering the various strategies and techniques discussed throughout this essay, individuals can develop their conversational skills and become effective communicators. It is important to remember that being a good conversationalist goes beyond simply talking; it involves actively listening, empathizing, and showing genuine interest in others. By practicing active listening, individuals can create a supportive and engaging environment that encourages open and meaningful dialogue. Adapting to different communication styles and being mindful of non-verbal cues can further enhance one's ability to connect with others. Developing good conversational skills also requires self-awareness and the willingness to continually improve and learn from experiences. It is essential to recognize and address any negative communication habits or tendencies that may impede effective conversation. Embracing diversity and being open-minded can broaden one's perspective and allow for more enriching conversations. By valuing others' opinions and perspectives, individuals can foster an atmosphere of respect and inclusivity, which can lead to more productive and engaging conversations.

It is vital to practice tact and diplomacy when engaging in difficult conversations or disagreements. By approaching these situations with empathy, patience, and a focus on finding common ground, individuals can navigate challenging conversations in a respectful and constructive manner. Being a good conversationalist is a lifelong journey that requires continuous effort and practice. By implementing the strategies outlined in this essay, individuals can develop invaluable skills that can benefit them in all areas of life. Whether it is in personal relationships, professional settings, or even casual encounters, being able to engage in meaningful and effective conversations is a skill that is highly valued and sought after. By prioritizing genuine curiosity, active listening, and respect for others, individuals can create deeper connections, foster understanding, and contribute to a more harmonious and engaging social environment. Being a good conversationalist is not only about the words we speak but also about the impact we have on others. It is about forging connections, building trust and empathy, and Creating positive and transformative experiences through conversation. I encourage all individuals to embrace the art of conversation and commit themselves to continuous growth and improvement in this important area of their lives.

RECAP OF KEY POINTS DISCUSSED IN THE ESSAY

This essay has provided a comprehensive guide on how to be a good conversationalist. The key points discussed can be summarized as follows. Firstly, establishing a genuine interest in the other person is crucial. By actively listening and asking open-ended questions, individuals can show that they value the other person's thoughts and feelings. Secondly, non-verbal communication plays a significant role in effective conversations. Maintaining eye contact, using appropriate body language, and being aware of one's tone of voice are essential in conveying interest and respect. The essay emphasizes the importance of being present in the conversation, avoiding distractions, and focusing on the speaker. This allows for a deeper level of engagement and understanding. It is crucial to be mindful of one's own speaking habits, such as avoiding interrupting and dominating the conversation, as well as using clear and concise language. The essay highlights the significance of being sensitive to cultural differences, respecting diverse perspectives, and avoiding controversial topics that may hinder open and respectful dialogue. The essay emphasizes the value of practice and self-reflection. Engaging in conversations regularly and reflecting on areas of improvement can lead to the development of stronger conversational skills over time. Becoming a good conversationalist requires a combination of psychological and interpersonal skills. It involves genuine interest, active listening, non-verbal communication, mindful presence, speaking habits, cultural sensitivity, and continuous practice. By internalizing these key points and implementing them in everyday interactions, individuals can enhance their social and professional relationships, foster meaningful connections, and contribute to a more inclusive and understanding society.

IMPORTANCE OF BEING A GOOD CONVERSATIONALIST IN PERSONAL AND PROFESSIONAL CONTEXTS

In both personal and professional contexts, being a good conversationalist is of utmost importance.

One reason is that effective communication skills are crucial for building and maintaining relationships. Whether it is in personal relationships with friends and family or in professional situations with colleagues and clients, the ability to engage in meaningful conversations is an essential skill. A good conversationalist knows how to listen actively and attentively, allowing the other person to feel heard and understood. This shows respect and empathy towards the other person, fostering deeper connections and trust. Being a good conversationalist allows individuals to express themselves effectively. In personal contexts, this is important for sharing thoughts and feelings with loved ones, fostering emotional intimacy and support. In professional settings, effective communication allows individuals to articulate their ideas and opinions confidently, making a positive impression on colleagues and superiors. A good conversationalist is skilled at asking thoughtful questions. This not only helps to keep the conversation flowing but also demonstrates genuine interest in the other person's perspective. Asking open-ended questions invites the other person to share more about themselves and their experiences, creating a space for meaningful and engaging conversations. Being a good conversationalist in both personal and professional contexts allows individuals to navigate difficult conversations with grace and sensitivity. Conflict resolution is often required in various contexts, and having strong communication skills is crucial in resolving conflicts in a respectful and effective manner. A skilled conversationalist understands the importance of active listening, acknowledging the other person's viewpoint, and finding common ground. This ability not only strengthens relationships but also helps to create a collaborative and harmonious environment. Being a good conversationalist is particularly vital in professional contexts, as it can lead to career advancement. Engaging in effective and meaningful conversations with colleagues and superiors can help individuals gain recognition for their ideas and contributions. The ability to communicate persuasively and convincingly can be invaluable in negotiating, influencing decisions, and even closing important deals. Employers highly value individuals who possess excellent communication skills, as it contributes to a positive work culture and improved productivity. Being a good conversationalist is essential in both personal and professional contexts. It enables individuals to build and maintain meaningful relationships, express themselves effectively, ask thoughtful questions, navigate difficult conversations, and even advance their career. By honing their conversational skills, individuals can foster deeper connections, resolve conflicts amicably, and make a positive impact in their personal and professional lives.

ENCOURAGEMENT TO CONTINUE DEVELOPING AND HONING CONVERSATIONAL SKILLS IN ORDER TO CULTIVATE MEANINGFUL CONNECTIONS

In the art of conversation, there is always room for improvement and growth. It is not a skill that can be mastered overnight; rather, it requires practice, dedication, and a genuine desire to connect with others. It is essential to encourage individuals to continue developing and honing their conversational skills in order to cultivate meaningful connections. One way to encourage the development of conversational skills is by creating an atmosphere that promotes open and non-judgmental communication. Conversations should be seen as opportunities for learning and understanding, rather than as competitions or opportunities to showcase one's knowledge. By fostering an environment where individuals feel free to express their thoughts and opinions without fear of judgment, they will be more inclined to engage in conversations and practice their skills. Another aspect of cultivating meaningful connections through conversation is actively listening. It is not enough to simply hear the words being spoken; true connection occurs when one actively listens and seeks to understand the other person's perspective. This involves paying attention to both verbal and non-verbal cues, such as facial expressions and body language, in order to fully comprehend the message being conveyed. By encouraging individuals to be active listeners, they will not only improve their conversational skills but also create deeper connections with others. Establishing a sense of curiosity and a willingness to learn from others is crucial for developing conversational skills. The more one is open-minded and willing to explore different perspectives, the more enriching their conversations will be. Encouraging individuals to ask questions, seek clarification, and engage in meaningful discussions can foster a lifelong love for learning and understanding others. It is essential to emphasize the importance of practice when it comes to honing conversational skills. Just like any other skill, conversation requires regular practice to be refined and improved. By encouraging individuals to engage in conversations regularly, they will become more comfortable and adept at navigating various topics and situations. In addition to regular practice, seeking feedback from others can also be beneficial. Constructive criticism allows for self-reflection and growth, providing valuable insights into areas that need improvement. Acknowledging the role of vulnerability in conversation can inspire individuals to connect with others on a deeper level. Being vulnerable means being open and authentic, allowing oneself to be seen and understood by others. By encouraging individuals to embrace vulnerability in their conversations, they can foster genuine connections rooted in trust and understanding. Encouraging individuals to continue developing and honing conversational skills is paramount in cultivating meaningful connections. By creating an atmosphere of open communication, promoting active listening, fostering curiosity, emphasizing practice and feedback, and acknowledging the role of vulnerability, individuals can nurture their conversational abilities and forge deeper connections with others.

Conversation is an art that requires dedication, effort, and a genuine desire to connect, and its rewards are invaluable.

BIBLIOGRAPHY

Marcia Gentry. 'Enrichment Clusters.' A Practical Plan for Real-World, Student-Driven Learning, Joseph S. Renzulli, Routledge, 9/3/2021

Euben. 'Journeys to the Other Shore.' Pearson Education India, 9/1/2007

Nancy Carson. 'Psychosocial Occupational Therapy.' Elsevier Health Sciences, 11/14/2019

Roy Billinton. 'Reliability Evaluation of Power Systems.' Springer Science & Business Media, 3/9/2013

Janice Lee Mong Li. 'Database Systems for Advanced Applications.' 27th International Conference, DASFAA 2022, Virtual Event, April 11–14, 2022, Proceedings, Part III, Arnab Bhattacharya, Springer Nature, 4/22/2022

David Phillips. 'Diversification in Modern Language Teaching.' Choice and the National Curriculum, Caroline Filmer-Sankey, Taylor & Francis, 4/21/2023

Leslie Harper. 'How to Stay Informed.' The Rosen Publishing Group, Inc, 7/15/2014

Joanna Grace. 'Sharing Sensory Stories and Conversations with People with Dementia.' A Practical Guide, Jessica Kingsley Publishers, 5/21/2018

Shirleen Davies. 'MacLarens of Fire Mountain Historical Western Romance Series Books 1 - 3.' Avalanche Ranch Press LLC, 11/25/2015

Mike Ritland. 'Unfuck America.' A Respectful, Open-Minded Conversation, Mike Drop Media, 11/16/2021

Vironika Tugaleva. 'The Art of Talking to Yourself.' Self-Awareness Meets the Inner Conversation, Soulux Press, 6/15/2017

Olivier Serrat. 'Knowledge Solutions.' Tools, Methods, and Approaches to Drive Organizational Performance, Springer, 5/22/2017

Emily Rose. 'Feeling and Showing Empathy.' Cherry Lake Publishing, 1/1/2022

Daniel Wendler. 'Improve Your Social Skills.' CreateSpace Independent Publishing Platform, 9/12/2014

Warren Berger. 'A More Beautiful Question.' The Power of Inquiry to Spark Breakthrough Ideas, Bloomsbury Publishing USA, 3/4/2014

Terry Lee. 'Breakthrough Leadership.' How Leaders Unlock the Potential of the People They Lead, Trafford Publishing, 8/1/2019

Michael Ellsberg. 'The Power of Eye Contact.' Your Secret for Success in Business, Love, and Life, Harper Collins, 4/27/2010

Robert DiYanni. 'Encounters: Essays for Exploration and Inquiry.' Pat C. Hoy, McGraw-Hill Companies,Incorporated, 11/23/1999